BROOKS SHAW & SON

COOKBOOK

D1616715

Casey Jones Village
Jackson, Tennessee

PUBLISHER AND AUTHOR:
The Old Country Store
56 Casey Jones Lane
Casey Jones Village
Jackson, TN 38305
800-748-9588

Printed in the USA by

WIMMER
The Wimmer Companies
Memphis

First Edition 1986
Second Edition 1989
Third Edition 1993
Fourth Edition 1998
Library of Congress Catalog Card Number: 86-050882

INTERNATIONAL STANDARD BOOK NUMBER: 0-9637980-06

EDITOR'S NOTE

Dear Friends:

It's been a labor of love for me to help bring an Old Country Store Cookbook to reality. We're very proud of this — our very first cookbook — and think you'll be proud to have it in your family collection.

I'd like to thank the following people who helped me put the cookbook together:

    Anne L. Shaw — Co-Editor
    Deborah Shaw Laman — Editorial Copy Consultant
    Sandra Magee, Co-ordinator
    Lawrence Taylor, Co-ordinator

Your loving support and dedication was invaluable to me.

A special thank you to all our many contributors — store employees, famous Jacksonians, local and area friends and family — this is your cookbook. Enjoy! Special appreciation to my husband, Norwood, for his love and support on this project, and everything I do.

And thank you for the many years of support to the Old Country Store. May this cookbook be a special keepsake for your family for years to come.

    Sincerely,
    Joyce Jones

TABLE OF CONTENTS

BROOKS SHAW & SON OLD COUNTRY STORE

MISSION STATEMENT

Our mission is to serve the Lord God through our business and to apply His Biblical principles in the work place.

We will offer the highest quality service, food and gifts to everyone who enters our doors. We want our service to be such that every customer feels as welcomed guests in our home. We will accomplish this by providing personal attention and giving good measure at a fair price.

We are committed to preserving a special place in time surrounding the turn of the century general store and providing genuine southern hospitality.

We also have a special responsibility to each employee. As a key part of our business, we will work to develop the full potential of each person.

We are committed to excellence. The extent of our success depends on the service we give to our guests and our community.

DEDICATION STATEMENT

We humbly dedicate our business and all it represents to the glory of God through His Son, Jesus Christ.

"A good name is to be desired more than great riches."

Proverbs 22:1

"May we serve you daily in thy wisdom."

Psalms 90:1-2

"OUR GOAL" STATEMENT

It is our goal to preserve the many items of the past that were used or sold in the General Store of the turn-of-the-century, and operate the store in the old time tradition of giving good measure for a fair price with the understanding that the extent of one success depends on how well we serve others and our community. We hope you enjoy your visits and that our store is a genuinely happy part of the lives of all who enter its doors.

In Loving Memory of
BROOKS C. SHAW, FOUNDER
DEDICATED TO MOM'S HOMECOOKING
AND POP'S OLD COUNTRY STORE
1924 – 1971

HOW IT ALL CAME ABOUT

In 1957 at the age of 32, Brooks Shaw was general manager of the Kelly Foods Corporation when he suffered his first severe heart attack. After a lengthy recovery, he was advised by his doctor to develop a hobby to relieve tensions he faced while operating a successful food processing plant.

Paul Jobe of Sikeston, Missouri, a very good friend of Brooks Shaw's, gave him three items—a brass cash register, an apple peeler, and a coffee mill. Paul suggested that since Brooks was closely associated with the grocery business, and had even worked in one in his youth, collecting items that were used or sold in old country stores during the turn of the century would be a great hobby to pursue.

With the help of many friends, in just a few years Brooks had accumulated one of the finest collections of old country store memorabilia in the country. Being an unselfish man it wasn't enough just to own a collection, he felt it needed to be displayed where others could appreciate and enjoy it too. And so, the idea for BROOKS SHAW & SON OLD COUNTRY STORE was created and became a reality in April, 1965.

At 40, Brooks Shaw had moved to the top of Kelly Foods, Inc., as President and major stockholder. It was at the peak of his career that he was told to retire from his business or face the possibility of a fatal heart attack. In 1966 he sold Kelly Foods, Inc. and retired to his real estate interest, his love of people, and his hobby of collecting Old Country Store antiques. Six years later at the age of 46, a fatal heart attack took Brooks Shaw's life. However, Brooks' courage, positive outlook, and eternal faith remain with the BROOKS SHAW & SON OLD COUNTRY STORE.

The original Country Store print is available in limited edition four color prints in our gift shoppe.

A BIT OF HISTORY

BROOKS SHAW & SON OLD COUNTRY STORE began on Airways Boulevard at the Highway 45 By Pass, Jackson, Tennessee in April 1965. Mr. Norwood Jones, a native Jacksonian, opened the store as the original storekeeper. Beginning as a museum filled with over 15,000 antiques, and later a full operation store, ice cream parlor, and restaurant, it soon became known throughout the country as one of the most interesting places to visit. The Store has been written about in nationwide publications and news stories reaching many parts of the world. A rocking chair marathon in 1972 drew thousands, and national TV and radio covered the event. In the competition, Susan Eliff rocked for 125 hours and 40 minutes to break a world's record for a woman rocking in a rocking chair.

In April of 1978, BROOKS SHAW & SON OLD COUNTRY STORE opened in its current location in CASEY JONES VILLAGE. The Shaw family, Anne and her children, Clark and Deborah, then formed a new corporation with long-time friends and business associates, Norwood Jones and Lawrence Taylor. They continue to operate the Store with the Shaw family.

The outside of the new store was constructed to resemble the original store, especially the front of the main section. The nine large doors used throughout the store were originally in Edgewood, the antebellum home built before the Civil War which was located on South Fairground Street, in the present location of McMillan Towers. The brick floors in the store are from this home also.

The large posts on the front of the store were once lamp posts in Bemis, Tennessee. The staircase post and rail are from the old two-story Cochran Grocery that once stood on East Chester Street.

A nostalgic return to a typical turn-of-the-century southern General Store

JACKSON'S ORIGINAL
"OLD COUNTRY STORE"

BROOKS SHAW'S OLD COUNTRY STORE is proud to be a one–of–a–kind, home owned and operated family business serving guests from across America and around the world since 1965.

Founded by Brooks C. Shaw, The Old Country Store today is owned by Brooks' widow, Anne; children Clark and Deborah; and long–time friends and business associates Norwood Jones and Lawrence Taylor.

Filled with 15,000 turn-of-the-century southern country store antiques and a 500 seat restaurant, The Old Country Store offers a dining and shopping experience like no other in the United States.

Our restaurant serves three daily buffets, a complete menu, and a large soup, salad, potato and fruit bar. After dinner, treat yourself to a delicious dessert from our 1890's Ice Cream Parlor and Soda Shoppe.

Before leaving The Old Country Store you must visit our Gift Shoppe which feature thousands of antiques and specializes in beautiful traditional gifts and decorative accessories reminiscent of the South. Enjoy the best of old-fashioned candies, jellies, jams, Tennessee country hams and more.

So, experience one of the South's favorite restaurants and gift shops the next time you travel I-40 between Nashville and Memphis.

Browse through our 6,000 square-foot Gift, Confectionary, Collectibles and Souvenir Shoppe among 15,000 Southern country antiques.

THE 1890'S ICE CREAM PARLOR
AND SODA SHOPPE

A highlight of the 1890's Ice Cream Parlor and Soda Shoppe is the silver and marble soda fountain. This was obtained from the Gilliam family in Okolona, Mississippi and had been placed in their store in the late 1880's. As we understand it, there were only 75 of these built and only three left in existence today.

The Ice Cream Parlor and Soda Shoppe features many fabulous flavors of delicious ice cream and an extensive menu of fancy treats like hot fudge sundaes, shakes, sodas, floats, banana splits, and much more. We also have whole homemade pies available for you to take home, and a deli take-out service.

This is the area of The Old Country Store where you can just sit and remember and enjoy the old-fashioned desserts you had as a child. Come by for a visit and see why the 1890's Ice Cream Parlor and Soda Shoppe is such a special attraction in our store.

THE GIFT SHOPPE

Surrounded by thousands of antiques in a charming old-fashioned atmosphere, the Gift Shoppe at THE OLD COUNTRY STORE is one of the finest gift shoppes in the Mid-South. There are over 6,000 square feet filled with a beautiful selection of quality traditional gifts reminiscent of the South.

THE OLD COUNTRY STORE specializes in the Southern country look that never goes out of style. We offer charming baskets, brass candle holders, handpainted wood crafts, marbles, glassware and much more.

The true antique buff could spend hours browsing through the extensive collection of over 15,000 antiques. The Shaw family began antiquing through the Mid-South before the store opened in 1965 and has continued to do so through the years. Among the many items you will find are old-fashioned brand soaps, medicines, advertising signs, chicken dusters, and Tennessee pea pickers. We also offer various food products and turn-of-the-century artifacts. Be sure to look for the hog bladder filled with snuff and an unusual picture of George Washington in addition to many other rare and unique items in the store.

The beautiful wood display shelves along the wall of the Gift Shoppe are over 150 years old and were originally from Germany. Brooks Shaw found them in Memphis in the 1960's, and they are now one of the most prized possessions in the store.

Call us at (901) 668-1223 for more information.

Surrounded by thousands of antiques in an unforgettable southern country atmosphere, our Gift Shoppe's confectionery area is filled with an assortment of old-fashioned treats from homemade fudge, Tennessee country hams, mix-n-match barrels of candy and licorice to pickled eggs and much more.

THE CONFECTIONARY SHOPPE

This unique selection of confectionery gifts are found exclusively at Brooks Shaw's "one-of-a-kind" OLD COUNTRY STORE amidst a fascinating collection of over 15,000 antiques.

Custom-made Old Country Store Gift Baskets which feature Tennessee food items may be shipped anywhere. They are always a hit with friends, family and customers or clients.

BROOKS SHAW'S
OLD COUNTRY STORE RESTAURANT

Southern country style buffets, a great salad bar, Tennessee country ham and white beans. . . sound delicious? Well, at Brooks Shaw's Old Country Store Restaurant we're proud to serve some of the finest southern cooking anywhere.

Three times a day we serve a delicious all-you-care-to-eat buffet: breakfast, lunch and dinner. We include a healthy salad, soup, potato and fruit bar with each buffet and add our signature hot kracklin' cornbread which is made right before your eyes on a real griddle. We also offer an extensive menu of great sandwiches and entrées.

Our 500-seat restaurant is as famous for its charm as it is for its cooking. Our Main Dining Room is decorated with checkered tablecloths and hundreds of antiques on the walls and hanging from the ceiling to delight you during your meal.

The Barnside Room is aptly named because of its southern barnwood walls and rustic atmosphere. It is our largest room and is perfect for tour groups and banquets.

The Heritage Room is full of patriotic and historic pictures and is dramatically enhanced by the red, white and blue star canopy hanging from the ceiling.

Upstairs at The Old Country Store, we host many private parties in both the Jones Room and the Taylor Room. Hundreds of private groups use our meeting rooms yearly, arranged by our Reservations and Groups Sales Department. From Christmas parties to club meetings, we can create a memorable atmosphere for your gathering.

The Old Country Store Restaurant is open from 6 a.m. to 10 p.m. daily except for Easter, Thanksgiving and Christmas Day.

HISTORIC CASEY JONES
HOME • RAILROAD MUSEUM • TRAIN STORE

Relive the days when the railroad was king. Browse through fascinating Casey Jones and railroad memorabilia, and tour the home of America's most famous railroad engineer, Jackson's own Casey Jones. Casey lived in this very home along with his wife and three children at the time of his fateful train crash in 1900. That train crash inspired the folk song, "The Ballad of Casey Jones" that immortalized Jonathan Luther "Casey" Jones in song and story to legendary status as an American folk hero.

Enjoy a tour of Casey Jones' Home where you can even climb aboard a 135 ton original steam locomotive like Casey's Ole No. 382 and ring the bell just like Casey. The official Gift Shoppe of the Home is the Casey Jones Train Store. It features Casey Jones and train theme gifts, toys, collectibles, music, books, as well as being an official dealer of Lionel, Brio and Thomas the Tank Engine. Enjoy two 25–foot model train exhibits sure to delight kids of all ages. All Aboard! Join us today! Open year round. Phone (901) 668-1222.

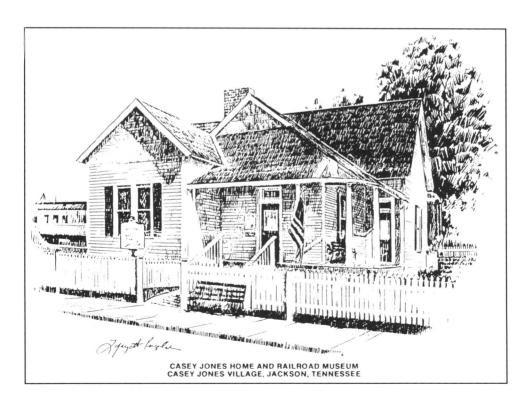

CASEY JONES HOME AND RAILROAD MUSEUM
CASEY JONES VILLAGE, JACKSON, TENNESSEE

The region's largest selection of train-themed gifts and toys, as well as model trains, are in the Casey Jones Train Store.

CASEY JONES STATION INN

A Legendary Night's Sleep!

Only steps away from Brooks Shaw's Old Country Store is our Casey Jones Station Inn, making Casey Jones Village a complete destination for you and your family. Over 50 beautifully decorated rooms welcome visitors from around the world with that genuine Southern hospitality we're famous for. And where else could you spend the night in a real caboose? Our 1890's railcar has been transformed into two beautiful connecting suites. All this makes staying at our Casey Jones Station Inn truly unforgettable. Enjoy the swimming pool and valuable meal and gift discounts to Brooks Shaw's Old Country Store Restaurant, Gift Shoppe, Ice Cream Parlor and Casey Jones Museum with your stay. Call 1-800-628-2812 for reservation information. Exclusively from the Casey Jones Station Inn.

CASEY JONES ADVENTURE GOLF

Enjoy a challenging and exciting game of miniature golf at Casey Jones Adventure Golf. This popular attraction is located here in Casey Jones Village and features two fun 18 hole courses the entire family can enjoy. (Seasonal) Call (901) 664-2755.

VISIT THE VILLAGE SHOPPES

Browse through these fine retail and specialty shoppes located here in Casey Jones Village! Alpine Christmas Gifts; Casey Jones Trading Post; Southern Magnolia; Wildlife n' Wood Studio; Casey Jones Adventure Golf; and coming soon Casey Jones Village Outdoor Music Theatre.

"CASEY JONES SPECIAL" MINIATURE TRAIN RIDE

"All Aboard" for kids and the kid at heart on the beautiful, restored train made in the early 1950's. Moves on a ¼ mile track. (Seasonal) Call (901) 668-1223.

Breads

Buttermilk Biscuits

2 C. plain flour
2 t. baking soda
¼ t. salt
1 C. buttermilk
2 T. shortening (lard makes them better)

Mix all dry ingredients well in a large bowl. Add buttermilk and shortening. Mix well until you have a fairly stiff dough. Empty on a well floured board and knead four or five times. Roll out to about ½ inch thick. Cut biscuits out and place in a well greased pan. Bake in 400° oven for 20–25 minutes.

Grandpa and Ramona Jones

Grandpa Jones

Grandpa Jones, whose banjo pickin' and humor made him a legend in his own time, was long a mainstay in the hearts of young and old alike. He was born Louis M. Jones in Niagra, Henderson County, Kentucky.

In 1935, Jones got a job with Bradley Kincaid in Clarksburg, West Virginia. The idea for the "Grandpa" image probably came when people began writing in asking his age. It seems he sounded older, especially on radio.

He joined the Grand Ole Opry in 1946, when he returned to the United States from serving in the Armed Forces in Germany. Grandpa also gained wide recognition as a star on the CBS-TV "HEE-HAW," which he called a good show that gave people the down-to-earth, clean and easy-to-associate-with type of entertainment that the typical TV watcher was looking for after a day of hard work.

Grandpa made about 200 appearances a year and was especially busy during the fall months playing state and county fairs, often sharing the stage with Roy Clark, co-star of "HEE-HAW." He also played colleges all over the country. The college audiences seem to accept his kind of music enthusiastically. His wife, Ramona, sometimes joined him on stage, playing the fiddle, for old-time country duets. He treated audiences to his classic version of "OLD RATTLER" and his famous Jimmy Rodger-style "Blue Yodeling." Since his great success on "HEE-HAW," audiences would often shout, "WHAT'S FOR SUPPER, GRANDPA?" to hear him give his rhymed recitation on the glories of ham-hocks and turnip-greens.

Grandpa lived on a farm outside Nashville until his death in 1998, where he raised registered Charlais "white" cattle, and was an avid hunter and fisherman. He and Ramona had three children: Eloise, Mark and Alisa.

Rolls

1 package yeast
1 t. salt
¼ C. lukewarm water
¾–1 C. water
¼ C. sugar
½ C. shortening
1 egg
2–3 C. flour

Dissolve 1 package yeast in ¼ C. lukewarm water. Cream ¼ C. sugar with ½ C. shortening. Add one egg; cream well. Add ¾–1 C. more warm water alternating with flour (approx. 2½ C.) to make stiff dough. Add salt. Set aside and let rise until double in bulk. Punch down. Set aside and let rise again. Then they are ready to roll out and cook.

Judy Haskins
In loving honor of Mrs. Ray Lasley (93)

Best Ever Hot Rolls

1 C. shortening
½ C. sugar
1 C. boiling water
1 C. cold water
2 packages dry yeast
6 C. unsifted plain flour
1 t. salt
2 eggs—beaten

Cream shortening and sugar. Slowly add boiling water. When shortening and sugar are mostly dissolved, add cup of cold water. When this mixture is lukewarm, add yeast. Allow to dissolve. Then add beaten eggs, flour and salt. Mix well. Place in refrigerator overnight. When ready to use, roll ½" thick, cut with biscuit cutter, butter with melted butter, fold over, re-butter, and place in warm (not drafty) place for 1½–2 hours. Bake 10–15 minutes or until brown at 400°.

Annie Louise Dent

Rolls

1 C. melted Crisco
¾ C. sugar
1½ t. salt
1 C. boiling water
2 beaten eggs
1 package yeast in 1 cup warm
   water
6 C. sifted flour

Mix first 4 ingredients. Cool and put in yeast and eggs together. Add 6 cups sifted plain flour 1 cup at a time. Mix and let dough rise. Roll out and cut and roll in melted butter. Let rise again. Bake in preheated 425° oven. Makes 12 servings.

Katherine Goodson

Rolls

1½ C. warm water
⅔ C. sugar
1½ t. salt
⅔ C. melted shortening
1 C. warm mashed potatoes
2 eggs—beaten
2 packages yeast
6 C. flour

Dissolve yeast in ½ cup warm water. Mix 1 cup water, sugar, salt, shortening, potatoes, and eggs. Add yeast. Add flour to make soft dough (about 3–4 cups). Cover in refrigerator 2 hours or overnight. Take out and work in rest of flour and make into rolls.

Joyce Jones

Ice Box Yeast Rolls

1 C. Shortening
½ C. sugar
1 T. salt
2 pkgs. yeast
2 eggs, beaten
6½–7 C. flour

Night before—Cream shortening, sugar, and salt. Add 1 C. hot water. Let cool. Add eggs. Dissolve 2 pkgs. yeast in one cup of tepid water. Add to above. Add flour. Stir well. Cover. Refrigerate up to one week.

Roll out on floured board, then cut. Dab butter on each roll. Let rise 2 hours. Bake at 400 degrees for 10–12 minutes.

Cinnamon Rolls

Use ½ above recipe. Roll into a rectangle. Brush with 4 to 6 T. of butter. Lavishly sprinkle with mixture of ¾ C. sugar and 4 t. cinnamon. Scatter ½ C. raisins. Role up, cut into half inch segments. Place in greased round cake pans. Brush with butter. Let rise 2 hours. Bake at 400 degrees for 10–12 minutes. Makes 16 rolls.

Donna Hewitt

Parker House Rolls

½ C. Crisco
2 C. milk
½ C. sugar
1 package yeast
½ C. water
Flour

Heat Crisco in sauce pan, add milk and sugar to lukewarm milk. Put yeast in water, add enough flour to make a runny dough. Let rise to double in size. Add 1 t. each of soda, salt, and baking powder to enough flour to make a stiff dough. Let rise and refrigerate and bake at 450° for 10–12 minutes.

Spoon Rolls

1 package dry yeast
2 C. lukewarm water
½ C. sugar
1 egg
½ C. melted shortening
4 C. sifted self-rising flour

Put 1 cup water in bowl and sprinkle yeast. Add second cup water. Add egg, sugar and shortening and then flour. Mix well and spoon into greased muffin pans. Bake at 400° for 20 to 25 minutes or until brown.

Easy Rolls

1 C. self-rising flour
2 T. mayonnaise
½ C. milk

Mix and bake in greased muffin pans at 400° for 12 minutes. Makes 6 servings.

Yeast Bread

½ C. boiling water
½ C. sugar
¾ C. Crisco
1½ t. salt
2 eggs
6 C. plain flour
1 C. lukewarm water
2 packages dry yeast

Dissolve yeast in lukewarm water. Mix boiling water, sugar, Crisco, and salt; let cool. Add eggs and 3 C. flour and yeast mixture. Add extra flour until you can knead on board. Let rise in bowl until double in size. Push down. Divide into 3 loaves. Let rise in loaf pan until double in size. Begin baking in cold oven. Bake 30 minutes at 350°. Makes 3 large or 5 small loaves.

Hon. Bob Conger
Mayor of Jackson

J. P.'s Cornbread

1 C. self-rising cornmeal
1 C. self-rising flour
1½ C. sweet milk
¼ C. buttermilk
¼ C. vegetable oil
2 eggs—beaten
2 T. brown sugar

Combine all ingredients, mixing well. Melt 1 to 2 T. shortening in a 10-inch cast iron skillet. Bake at 450° for 25–25 minutes.

Juanita Shaw

Beefie Jalapeno Cornbread

1 C. meal
1 C. buttermilk
2 eggs
¾ t. salt
½ t. soda
½ C. salad oil
17 oz. can cream style corn
1 lb. ground beef
1 C. American cheese—shredded
1 medium onion—chopped
4 or 5 hot peppers

Combine all ingredients except beef and cheese. Set aside. Brown beef and drain. Pour ½ of cornmeal mixture in well-greased pan (13 x 9 x 2). Place meat on top of mixture, place cheese on top of meat. Pour rest of cornmeal mixture in pan and bake at 350° for 50 minutes.

Georgie Mallard

Breads

Cornbread Stuffing

3 C. slightly dry bread crumbs
5 C. coarsely crumbled corn bread
1 t. poultry seasoning
1 t. salt
Dash of pepper
1 C. finely chopped celery
½ C. finely chopped onion
½ C. butter
2 beaten eggs
¼ C. chicken broth or water

Toss together breads and other seasonings. Cook celery and onion in butter until tender but not brown. Pour over bread. Add eggs and toss lightly to mix. Moisten with broth and toss. Enough for a 10 lb. turkey or cook about 30 minutes in 9 x 12 pan.

Georgie Mallard

Cornbread-Crouton Dressing

¼ C. butter
1 C. chopped celery
1 chopped onion
3 C. herb-seasoned croutons
3 C. cornbread crumbs
2 t. poultry seasoning
1 t. black pepper
2 cans condensed broth or liquid
    from cooked giblets
6 eggs—boiled
2 cans Cream of Chicken soup

Saute celery and onion in butter; add all of the other ingredients and place in a large casserole and bake at 400° until lightly browned on top. (If the dressing is not almost soupy when you mix it together, add more liquid so it won't be so dry when it is baked.)

Dolly Mathis

Hush Puppies

1 C. self-rising corn meal
¾ C. self-rising flour
⅓ C. sugar
1 egg
4 T. chopped onion
½ C. sweet milk
2 T. Jalapeno pepper
½ C. whole kernel corn—drained

Mix dry ingredients together. Add egg and milk. Mix well. Add onion, corn, and pepper. Stir until well mixed. Drop by spoonfuls into hot, deep fat. Fry to golden brown and drain on paper towels. Makes about 2 dozen.

Sue Woods

Mexican Corn Bread

1 large onion
2 eggs
½ C. Wesson oil
1 hot pepper
1 C. cream-style corn
8 oz. sour cream
1½ C. self-rising corn meal mix
4 oz. sharp cheddar cheese—
   grated

In blender, process onion, eggs, oil, and pepper; blend well. In bowl, mix corn and sour cream with corn meal and ingredients from blender. In hot, greased skillet, pour in half of mixture, cover with ¾ of the grated cheddar, pour rest of cornmeal mixture in and top with remaining cheese. Bake at 400° until done.

Annie Lee Lasley

Bride's Cornbread

1 C. self-rising cornmeal
1 C. self-rising flour
1 C. milk
1 egg

Mix all ingredients and pour into hot, well-greased iron skillet. Cook at 450° for 12–15 minutes until crisp and brown.

Shirley Droke

Hush Puppies

8 T. meal
2 T. plain flour
1 egg
Garlic salt (to taste)
Onion powder (to taste)
Pepper (to taste)
2 T. cooking oil
Milk to consistency

Mix ingredients together and deep fry by spoons full.

Melinda Wilkins

Corn Light Bread

2 C. plain corn meal
¾ C. plain flour
1 t. soda
1 T. salt
1 C. sugar
2 C. buttermilk
4 T. butter—melted

Sift together, add buttermilk and melted butter. Mix. Grease loaf pan, sprinkle bottom of pan with small amount of corn meal. Pour in mixture. Bake at 300° for 1 hour.

Mrs. V. L. Taylor

Breads

Quick Corn Light Bread

2 C. corn meal—plain
½ C. flour—plain or all purpose
¾ C. sugar
1 t. soda
1 t. salt
1 t. active dry yeast
2 C. buttermilk
3 T. Crisco—melted

Mix and sift first 5 ingredients. Mix lightly with all ingredients. Pour in greased loaf pan and bake at 375° about 55 minutes.

Rebecca Porter

Corn Fritters

2 eggs
¾ C. milk
2½ C. self-rising flour
1 t. salt
1 T. sugar
2 T. melted butter
1 #2 can of cream style corn
1 #2½ can sliced pineapple
2 C. Crisco oil
Red currant jelly

Beat eggs slightly. Add milk, flour, sugar, butter & corn, salt; beat until well mixed. Drop by spoonfulls into hot, deep oil (375°). Fry 3–4 minutes until golden brown. Drain on absorbent paper towel. Place on a slice of pineapple; top with cube of red currant jelly and serve with chicken or ham. Yields 18 large or 24 small.

Lucille O. Johnson

Spoon Bread

2 C. milk
1 C. cornmeal
1 t. salt
2 T. butter or margarine
1 t. sugar
3 eggs—beaten
1 C. milk

Heat milk in saucepan; stirring, add cornmeal. Cook until a mush. Add salt, butter, sugar, eggs, and 1 C. milk. Mix well. Pour in a greased 2 quart casserole dish. Bake at 325° for 1–1½ hours.

Hon. Bob Conger
Mayor of Jackson

Spoon Bread

1 C. yellow cornmeal
3 C. milk
2 T. salad oil
1 t. baking powder
1 t. salt
3 eggs—separated and well-beaten

Cook cornmeal and 2 C. milk in saucepan until it has the consistency of mush. Remove from heat; stir in 1 C. milk, salad oil, baking powder, and 1 t. salt. Add the beaten egg yolks; fold in stiffly beaten egg whites. Pour spoon bread mixture into a greased 1½ quart casserole dish. Bake at 325° for 1 hour. Serves 6–8.

Pauline (Polly) Long

Apple Muffins

2 C. flour
½ t. salt
4 t. baking powder
¼ C. sugar
¾ t. cinnamon
¼ t. nutmeg
1 egg—beaten
1 C. milk
⅓ C. oil
¾–1 C. apple—peeled and chopped

Combine dry ingredients.
Combine egg, milk, and oil; add to dry ingredients. Stir just to moisten, add apple and mix. Fill greased muffin tins ⅔ full. Bake at 350° for 25 minutes. Serve with honey.

Karen Hewitt Wimpee

Sweet Potato Biscuits

4 C. flour
¾ C. shortening
¾ C. sugar
1 t. salt
3 t. baking powder
3 medium sweet potatoes
1½ C. buttermilk
1 t. soda

Boil sweet potatoes with jackets on, then peel and mash. Sift flour, baking powder, salt, and sugar in bowl; then add shortening, and sweet potatoes. Roll out and cut with biscuit cutter. Bake in 400° oven until brown. Serve hot with butter for breakfast.

Ann & Josephine Tanner

Breads

Donnie's Homemade Biscuits

2 C. self-rising flour
¼ cup shortening
¾ C. buttermilk

Preheat oven to 450°.
Cut shortening into flour, add milk. Turn out dough onto lightly floured board and knead until smooth. Roll dough ½ inch thick and cut with 2 inch biscuit cutter. Place biscuits onto lightly greased pan. Bake 10 to 12 minutes or until brown. Makes 12 to 14 biscuits.

Donnie Newble

Cinnamon Blitz

1 8 oz. package cream cheese
1½ C. sugar
1 stick butter (melted)
1 egg yolk
2 T. cinnamon
1 loaf bread

Mix cream cheese and 1 C. of sugar and egg yolk. Trim crust off of bread and roll each slice very thin with rolling pin. Mix ½ C. sugar and cinnamon in separate bowl. Spread cream cheese mixture on slice of bread and roll up — jelly roll style. Dip in melted butter and then roll in cinnamon and sugar mixture. Place on cookie sheet and freeze.
Bake in a 375° oven for 15 minutes.

Leigh Ann Jones Taylor

Tennessee Pumpkin Bread

3⅓ C. sifted self-rising flour
1 t. cinnamon
1 t. nutmeg
⅔ C. shortening
2⅔ C. sugar
¼ t. vanilla
4 eggs
2 C. canned mashed pumpkin
⅔ C. water
1 C. chopped pecans or walnuts

Grease 2 loaf pans (9 x 5 x 3). Sift together flour, cinnamon, nutmeg. In another mixing bowl, cream shortening, sugar and vanilla. Add eggs, one at a time, beating thoroughly after each one. Stir in pumpkin, stir in dry ingredients in four additions, alternating with water until just smooth, do ot over-beat. Bake at 350° for 45–55 minutes or until knife inserted in center comes out clean.

Dolly Mathis

Oatmeal Bread

1¼ C. sifted flour
¾ C. sugar
1 t. salt
1 t. baking powder
1 t. soda
½ t. cinnamon
¼ t. nutmeg
1 C. quick cooking oats
½ C. raisins
1¼ C. applesauce
⅓ C. salad oil
2 lg. eggs
¼ C. milk

Topping:

2 T. brown sugar
2 T. pecans
¼ t. cinnamon

Sift, flour, sugar, salt, and other spices. Stir in oats and raisins. Mix other items together in small bowl and beat with fork. Pour into dry mixture. Sprinkle with topping. Bake at 350° for 55–60 minutes. Serves 10.

Norma Taylor

Zucchini Bread

2 C. shredded zucchini
1 3 oz. can pineapple—drained
3 eggs
1 C. oil
2 C. sugar
3 C. self rising flour
½ t. cinnamon
2 t. vanilla
Chopped nuts (optional)

Beat eggs. Add sugar, oil, and vanilla until creamy. Add rest of ingredients and nuts last if desired. Bake in 2 long baking dishes 1 hour at 350°.

Georgie Mallard

Honey Wheat Bread

1½ C. water
1 C. cottage cheese
½ C. honey
¼ C. margarine
4½ C. all purpose flour
2 C. wheat flour
2 T. sugar
3 t. salt
2 packages dry yeast
1 egg

Heat first 4 ingredients until very warm. Combine this warm liquid with 2 cups flour and remaining ingredients. Beat 2 minutes. Stir in remaining flour to make stiff dough. Knead until smooth and elastic. Put in greased bowl and let rise until double. Punch down and divide into 2 loaves or 24 rolls. Let rise again until double. Bake at 350° until golden brown and sounds hollow on top. Brush the warm loaves with honey and butter mix.

Georgie Mallard

Breads

Poppy Seed Bread

3 C. all-purpose flour
2 C. sugar
3 eggs
¾ C. vegetable oil
1½ C. milk
1½ T. poppy seeds
1½ t. baking powder
1½ t. salt
1½ t. vanilla extract
1½ t. almond extract
1½ t. butter flavoring

Combine all ingredients in a large bowl; beat 2 minutes at medium speed with electric mixer. Spoon batter into 2 greased and floured 8 x 4 x 3 inch loaf pans. Bake at 350° for 1 hour or until a wooden pick inserted in center comes out clean. Cool loaves in pans 10 minutes; remove from pans and cool completely on wire racks.

Forest Heights United Methodist Church

Holiday Bread

1 lb. dates or ½ lb. dates and ½ lb. raisins
7 oz. coconut
2 C. sugar
3 sticks margarine
2 t. cinnamon
½ t. cloves
½ t. ginger
1 t. salt
1 t. nutmeg
3 t. red food coloring
2 t. soda
2 C. nuts
2 jars marachino cherries
3 slices candied pineapple
¼ lb. each red and green candied cherries
3 C. flour
2 t. baking powder
3 lg. eggs

Boil together first 10 ingredients. Remove from heat. Stir in 2 t. soda. Beat hard. Cool. Add remaining ingredients and bake in tube pan at 275° for 2–2½ hours.

Fred Hunke

Breads

Six Week Bran Muffins

3 C. Raisin Bran
½ C. Crisco—melted and cooled
1½ C. sugar
2 C. buttermilk
2½ C. flour
2 t. soda
1 t. salt
2 eggs

Mix dry ingredients, add eggs, melted Crisco, and buttermilk. Store in covered container in refrigerator for 24 hours before using. When using, *do not stir.* Will keep for six weeks. Bake at 400° about 20 minutes. Makes approximately 30.

Virginia L. Sculley

Lemon Muffins

½ C. shortening
½ C. sugar
2 egg yolks—beaten
¼ C. lemon juice
1 C. all-purpose flour
½ T. salt
1 T. baking powder
2 egg whites—beaten stiff
½ lemon rind—grated

Cream shortening and sugar until smooth. Add egg yolks and beat well. Add lemon juice alternately with flour (sifted with baking powder and salt. Mix lightly after each addition. Fold in beaten egg whites and grated lemon rind. Fill greased muffin rings ⅔ full and bake in moderate 350° oven 20 minutes. Serves 8.

Mrs. Ray Lasley

Apple Fritters

1 egg
½ C. milk
1 T. shortening
1 C. diced apples
1 C. flour
1 T. sugar
1 t. baking powder
¼ t. salt

Beat egg and milk together. Add the 1 T. melted shortening and the apples. Combine the dry ingredients and add to egg mixture. Mix well. Drop from tablespoon into deep fryer heated to 375°. Cook about 4–5 minutes until brown. Place on paper towel to drain. Roll in confectioners sugar. Makes 1½ dozen.

Geni Holmes

Banana Nut Bread

2 eggs
1 C. sugar
½ C. oil
⅓ C. water
1¾ C. plain flour
1 t. soda
½ t. salt
3 mashed bananas (very ripe)
½ C. chopped pecans

Mix all ingredients with a spoon. Grease and flour loaf pan. Bake in a 350° oven for 45 minutes.

Norma Taylor

J. P.'s Cornbread II

1½ C. self-rising cornmeal
½ C. self-rising flour
1½ C. milk
¼ C. buttermilk
½ C. vegetable oil
1 egg, beaten
¼ C. sugar

Combine all ingredients, mixing well. Heat skillet in oven with 1 to 2 T. of shortening until shortening melts and sizzles when a drop of mixture is dropped in the skillet. Pour mixture in skillet and bake at 450° for 20-25 minutes. Make sure center is done by touch or straw test. Mixture will also make 12 muffins.

Juanita Shaw

Mexican Cornbread

1½ C. self-rising cornmeal
3 eggs
1 C. cream style corn
⅔ C. cooking oil
1 C. buttermilk
1 large hot pepper (chopped)
1 small onion (chopped)
1 green bell pepper (chopped)
1 C. sharp cheddar cheese
Salt to taste

Cook until golden brown at 350°.

Maxine Crumby

Salads

Salads

Cole Slaw for a Great Big Picnic

10 large heads fresh cabbage—
    chopped finely
10 large green bell peppers—
    chopped finely
10 C. apple cider vinegar
10 C. sugar
10 T. mustard seed
10 T. tumeric
10 T. salt
10 T. celery seed

Mix vinegar, sugar, mustard seed, tumeric, salt, and celery seed thoroughly and heat to boiling point. While hot, pour over cabbage and pepper mixture and mix all thoroughly. Chill and serve. Serves 120–150.

Fresh Broccoli Salad

1 bunch fresh broccoli
3 eggs—hard boiled
4 green onion tops—chopped
½ lb. bacon—cooked and crumbled
½ C. green olives—chopped
½ C. mayonnaise
1 8 oz. bottle Wish Bone Italian
    dressing

Just before ready to serve, toss broccoli, eggs, onion, bacon, and olives with a mixture of ½ C. mayonnaise and Italian dressing. Be sure to use mayonnaise and not salad dressing.

Deborah Shaw Laman

Broccoli Salad

1 bunch broccoli—chopped
1 medium purple onion—chopped
10 slices bacon—fried and
    crumbled
½ C. raisins

Toss together broccoli, onion, bacon, and raisins. Mix topping and pour over all. Refrigerate until ready to serve.

Dot Simpson

Topping:

1 C. mayonnaise
½ C. sugar
2 T. vinegar

Salads

Spinach Salad

1 lb. fresh spinach
1 C. watercress
1 lb. sliced mushrooms
1 medium red onion—thinly sliced
1 lb. bacon—fried, drained, and
    chopped
3 eggs—boiled and sliced

Tear greens into bite sized pieces; toss with mushrooms and onions. Put in salad bowl, sprinkle with bacon and boiled eggs.

Marjorie Schrivner

Twenty-Four Hour Salad

1 head lettuce
1 onion, sliced (small-medium)
1 lb. fried, crumbled bacon
1 head cauliflower
¼ C. sugar
2 C. mayonnaise
⅓ C. Parmesan cheese
Salt and pepper to taste

Layer in the above order. Cover tightly and refrigerate overnight. Toss and serve.

Glenna Yoder

Cherry Cream Freeze Salad

1 15 oz. can Eagle Brand milk
1 1 lb. 5 oz. can cherry pie filling
¼ t. almond extract
¼ C. lemon juice
¾ C. or 1 9 oz. can crushed
    pineapple (well drained)
2 C. heavy whipped cream

Combine first 5 ingredients and mix. Fold in whipped cream. Put in 9 x 5 x 3 inch loaf pan, cover tightly and freeze 24 hours or until very firm. Slice to serve.

Gloria J. Roberts

Sauerkraut Salad

1 can sauerkraut—drained
1 medium carrot—grated
½ medium onion—chopped or
    grated
½ medium green pepper—chopped
    or grated
Pimento may be added or
    substituted
⅓ C. sugar
⅓ C. oil
½ t. celery seed

Rinse sauerkraut with cold water, allow to stand, draining off water. Mix sugar, oil, and celery seed. Pour over vegetables and toss lightly.

Kay Henson

Congealed Vegetable Salad

1 package lemon jello
1½ C. hot water
2 t. vinegar
1 t. salt
1 small can English peas
1 small can pimento
1 C. celery—chopped
2 bell peppers
1 small bottle sweet pickles

Dissolve jello in hot water, vinegar, and salt; refrigerate. When begins to thicken, add peas, pimento, celery, peppers and pickles. Put in mold and chill until set.

Marjorie Lasley Scott

Vegetable Salad

1 bunch broccoli (use flowerets)
1 cauliflower
3 carrots—sliced very thin
1 small onion—sliced thin
Pinch of salt
⅔ C. mayonnaise
⅓ C. oil
¼ C. sugar
½ C. apple cider vinegar

Mix mayonnaise, oil, sugar, and vinegar. Pour over vegetables, chill for 2–3 hours.

Annie Lee Lasley

Salads

Kraut Slaw

1 small can kraut—drained
¾ C. sugar
¾ C. vinegar
1 C. chopped onion
1 C. celery—chopped
2 T. pimento

Bring sugar and vinegar to boil. Let cool, mix with kraut, adding onion, celery, and pimento. Mix all together and serve.

Eleanor Haskins

Congealed Potato Salad

2 C. diced potatoes—cooked
2 C. diced celery
2 T. chopped pimento
1 small can ripe olives—chopped
½ pint sour cream
¼ C. green onions—chopped
3 eggs—hard boiled
1 envelope Knox gelatin
¼ C. cold water
1 C. mayonnaise
3 T. Kraft French dressing

Slice eggs and marinate in French dressing. Soften gelatin in cold water and dissolve over hot water. When cool, add to mayonnaise. Add sour cream, vegetables, and eggs, and salt and pepper to taste. Mix well. Put in square or oblong pan and chill thoroughly. Serves 8.

Margaret Hewitt

Macaroni and Cheese Salad

3 oz. 7 minute macaroni—cooked, drained, cooled
1 C. cubed sharp cheddar cheese
½ C. diced celery
⅓ C. diced green pepper
¼ C. green onion tops—chopped
2 T. pimento—chopped
¼ C. drained pickle relish
½ C. salad dressing
1 T. mustard
¼ t. salt

Blend all ingredients. May be refrigerated.

Bonnie Cummings

Slaw

1 C. dark vinegar
½ C. sugar
¾ C. Wesson oil
1 T. salt
1 T. celery seed
1 T. dry mustard
1 large cabbage—chopped
1 large onion—chopped
2 carrcts—grated
1 large bell pepper—chopped

Mix cabbage, onion, carrots and pepper in large bowl. Heat remaining ingredients to a boil. Reduce heat and simmer 5 minutes. Pour over cabbage mixture. Refrigerate covered.

This will keep a week to 10 days in the refrigerator. This should be made the day before to let the ingredients blend well to improve the flavor.

Celia Ward Collins

Creamy Italian Dressing

1 8 oz. package cream cheese
¼ C. vinegar
1 T. dillseed
1 envelope Good Season Salad
    Dressing Mix
1 C. sour cream
1 T. chives
1 T. mayonnaise
1 C. salad oil

Whip first four ingredients. Fold in remaining ingredients. This dressing can be made ahead of time and will keep for weeks.

Marjorie Schrivner

Cold Spiced Fruit

1 20 oz. can pineapple chunks
1 16 oz. can sliced peaches
1 16 oz. can apricot halves
1 29 oz. can pears
1 C. sugar
½ C. vinegar
3 sticks cinnamon
5 whole cloves
1 3 oz. package cherry Jello

Drain fruit well. Reserve all pineapple juice and ½ of peach and apricot juice. Combine juices with sugar, vinegar, spices, and Jello. Simmer 30 minutes. Add juices to fruit while hot and let set for 24 hours in refrigerator. Serve chilled.

Elizabeth & Mildred Harris

Pear Salad

1 3 oz. package lime Jello
1 8 oz. package cream cheese
1 large can pears
1 medium Cool Whip
1 C. pecans—chopped

Dissolve Jello in heated pear juice, adding water to make 1¾ C. liquid. Cool. Mix softened cream cheese with pears, cut fine. Add jello mixture, mix well. Add nuts, return to refrigerator and when slightly congealed, fold in Cool Whip and pour into 9 x 13 inch dish.

Anne & Frances Tanner

Cherry Congealed Salad

2–3 oz. packages cherry Jello
2 C. hot water
1 large can crushed pineapple not drained
1 jar cherry pie filling
8 oz. Philadelphia Cream cheese
½ C. sugar
8 oz. sour cream
1 t. vanilla

Dissolve Jello in water. Add pineapple with juice and pie filling. Chill until firm. Mix thoroughly cream cheese, sour cream, sugar and vanilla with electric mixer. Pour over congealed Jello mixture.

Susie B. Lasley

Delicious 24-Hour Salad

1 #303 can pitted Royal Ann cherries
1 #303 can pineapple tidbits
½ lb. blanched almonds
1 lb. marshmallows—cut fine
4 egg yolks—beaten
½ t. salt
4 T. cornstarch
Juice of 1 lemon
2 C. heavy cream—whipped

Drain cherries and pineapple, saving juice. Measure juice, add water to make 1 C. Mix fruit, almonds, and marshmallows. Put juice in double boiler, heat. Mix egg yolks, salt, and cornstarch. Add to juice, cook, stirring until thick. Cool. Add lemon juice. Mix with marshmallow mixture. Let stand in refrigerator 24 hours. Fold in whipped cream before serving.
Serves 10–12.

Betty J. Lasley

24-Hour Salad

2 eggs—beaten
4 T. vinegar
4 T. sugar
2 T. butter
2 C. white cherries—halved
2 C. pineapple tidbits
2 C. oranges—cut up
2 C. miniature marshmallows
1 C. cream

Put eggs in double boiler and add vinegar and sugar, beating constantly until thick and smooth. Remove from heat, add butter and cool. When cold, fold in whipped cream and fruit mixture. Place in refrigerator for 24 hours. Serves 10–12.

Mildred Harris

24 Hour Frozen Fruit Salad

2 C. Royal Ann cherries—cut in
    halves
2 C. chunked pineapple
2 C. oranges—cut in pieces
2 C. marshmallows—chopped
1 C. whipping cream

Dressing to pour over fruit:

2 egg yolks—well beaten
4 T. vinegar
1 T. sugar
2 T. butter

Cook until thick. Mix with fruit and let set for 24 hours.

Serena Mitchell

Raspberry Salad

2 packages raspberry Jello
2 packages frozen raspberries—
    thaw and drain
1 small can pineapple chunks—
    drained
1 can applesauce
2 C. hot water
1 8 oz. cream cheese
1½ T. mayonnaise
1 T. milk

Dissolve Jello in hot water. Add 1 C. berry or pineapple juice (or mixed). Add applesauce. Let set until soft jelly stage. Add berries and pineapple. Served topped with cream cheese softened with mayonnaise and milk. Can add chopped nuts to topping.

Mrs. Ira Johnson

Pistachio Salad

1 box Royal pistachio pudding mix
1 20 oz. can crushed pineapple—
    not drained
½ C. miniature marshmallows
½ C. chopped nuts
1 small box Cool whip

Put undrained pineapple in bowl and mix with pudding mix. Stir well. Add with marshmallows and nuts. Fold in Cool Whip.

Rebecca Porter

Strawberry Salad

2 packages strawberry jello
2½ C. boiling water
1 small package frozen
    strawberries
3 bananas—sliced
½ C. chopped pecans (optional)
½ pint sour cream

Dissolve gelatin in boiling water. Add stawberries and stir until thawed. Add sliced bananas and chopped pecans. Pour half of mixture into 8 x 8 x 2 pan and hold in refrigerator until firm. Jell remaining half only to thick pouring consistency. Spread sour cream on first mixture and pour remaining half on top. Place in refrigerator to jell entire mixture.

Kay Henson

Strawberry Salad

2 boxes strawberry jello
⅔ C. sugar
2 C. hot water
8 oz. cream cheese
9 oz. Cool Whip
8 oz. crushed pineapple, drained
½ C. pecans—chopped

Mix jello, sugar, and water and let almost gel. Mix remaining ingredients together and then add to jello. Refrigerate.

Diane Crouch

Stained Glass Salad

1 can peach pie filling
1 pint strawberries
1 can mandarin oranges
1 large can pineapple chunks
2 bananas—sliced and coated in
    lemon juice

Mix together and refrigerate.

Sandra Magee

Easy Cranberry Salad

1 package orange jello
1 package raspberry jello
2 C. boiling water
1 15 oz. can crushed pineapple—
  undrained
1 can whole cranberry sauce
½ C. chopped pecans

Dissolve jello in boiling water. Let chill in refrigerator. Remove and add remaining ingredients. Place back in refrigerator for congealing.

Deborah Shaw Laman

Cranberry Salad

2 C. cranberries
1 C. pecans
1 C. sugar
1 orange
1 apple
1 small can crushed pineapple
  drained
1 package lemon jello

Remove seeds from orange and core from apple. Run berries, orange and apple through food chopper. Mix sugar with pineapple and combine with ground ingredients. Add nuts. Add all to jello and turn into molds.

Anne L. Shaw

Pineapple Cranberry Salad

1 #2 can crushed pineapple
2 small packages lemon jello
½ C. lemon juice
½ C. chopped nuts
2 cans whole cranberry sauce

Drain syrup from pineapple and add enough water to make 1½ C. liquid. Heat to boiling and add to jello. Stir until completely dissolved. Stir in pineapple, lemon juice, nuts and cranberry sauce. Pour into an oiled 8″ ring mold or an 8 x 10 pyrex bowl. Chill until firm.

Celia Willard Collins

Blueberry Salad

2 3 oz. packages mixed fruit Jello
2 C. boiling water
1 15 oz. can plain blueberries
1 8 oz. can crushed pineapple
1 8 oz. cream cheese
½ C. sugar
½ pint sour cream
1 t. vanilla

Dissolve Jello in water. Drain pineapple and blueberries and add 1 C. of drained liquid to the jello. Stir in drained pineapple and blueberries. Pour into 2 quart dish and let set until firm. Mix together softened cream cheese, sour cream, sugar, and vanilla. Spoon over blueberry mixture and refrigerate.

Sandra Magee

Georgie's Fruit Salad

1 large can fruit cocktail
1 medium can chopped pineapple
3 oranges—peeled and chunked
½ package of mini marshmallows
½ pint sour cream
¼ C. coconut

Mix together. Chill and serve.

Georgie Mallard

Apple Salad

1 large red apple, unpeeled and
　　diced
1 large golden apple, unpeeled and
　　diced
1 8 oz. can pineapple chunks,
　　drained
1 C. miniature marshmallows
⅔ C. flaked coconut
½ C. chopped pecans
¼ C. raisins
2 T. chopped celery
⅓ C. mayonnaise

Mix all ingredients, cover and refrigerate. Looks pretty served in a glass trifle bowl.

Sandra Magee

Holiday Salad

1 package strawberry gelatin
1½ C. water
1 small can crushed pineapple

Dissolve gelatin in 1 C. hot water; add ½ C. cold water and pineapple. Pour into large ring mold which has been greased with butter. Chill until firm.

1 8 oz. package cream cheese
1 C. cream
1 package lemon gelatin
1 C. hot water

Mix cream cheese with cream. Dissolve gelatin in water. Combine with cheese mixture. Pour over strawberry layer in ring mold. Chill until firm.

1 package lime gelatin
1½ C. water
1 small can pears

Dissolve gelatin in 1 C. hot water, add ½ C. cold water and pears. Pour over cheese layer in mold. Chill until firm, then unmold.

You will have a red, white, and green salad. Fill center with dressing of your choice. Serves 10–12.

Anne L. Shaw

Fruit Mold

18 lg. marshmallows
3 T. pineapple juice
1 8 oz. package cream cheese
1 lg. can fruit cocktail—drained
1 lg. can pineapple chunks
½ C. nuts—chopped

Place marshmallows and juice over low heat until marshmallows are melted. Have cream cheese at room temperature. Beat until fluffy. Add marshmallow mixture and blend. Add fruit and nuts, pour in dish or mold and refrigerate.

Sharon Deaton

Green Salad Mold

8 oz. cream cheese
1 large can pears
1 small package lime jello
1 package Dream Whip
1 C. pear juice

Heat pear juice and add to jello. Put aside until set. Mash pears and cream cheese. Mix everything. Fold in prepared Dream Whip.

Marty Langdon

Salads

Congealed Fruit Salad

1 small can sliced pineapple—
   drained
½ lb. marshmallows—cut up
1 large can white cherries—drained
1 C. pecans—broken
½ pint cream—beaten stiff

Use all the juice from the pineapple and ½ C. of the cherry juice and heat but not boil. Add this to the cut marshmallows and beat until fluffy. Add 1 t. gelatin, soaked in ¼ C. water, to this. Add other ingredients, folding in cream last. Chill and serve on lettuce. Serves 4–6.

Alma Lawrence

Holiday Cranberry Relish

3 apples
3 oranges—peeled, seeded
1 lb. fresh cranberries
1 C. pecan pieces
1 orange rind—grated
2 C. sugar

Grind apples, cranberries, and oranges in blender. Combine with remaining ingredients and let set in refrigerator 2–3 days before serving. This relish keeps well for several weeks. Will serve more than one holiday gathering.

Mary Frances Buntin Wadley

Quick Spiced Peach Halves

1 can (30 oz.) cling peach halves
¼ C. sugar
¼ C. white vinegar
1 stick cinnamon
5–6 cloves

Drain peaches. Add remaining ingredients to peach syrup and boil 2–4 minutes. Pour at once over peach halves. Let stand overnight. Drain well and serve.

Alma Lawrence

Buttermilk Salad

1 large peach Jello
1 medium can crushed pineapple
2 C. buttermilk
8 oz. Cool Whip
1 C. nuts

Heat pineapple and add jello. Stir until mixed. Add all other ingredients. Chill.

Rebecca Porter

Frozen Cranberry Salad

1 16 oz. can whole cranberry sauce
1 14 oz. can sweetened condensed milk
1 20 oz. can crushed pineapple, well drained
¼ C. lemon juice
½ C. chopped pecans
12 oz. Cool Whip—thawed

Mix all together until well blended. Pour into 9 x 13 inch glass dish. Freeze.

Note: This is wonderful frozen in paper lined muffin tins. Will make 24. After frozen, place in ziploc bag and use whenever desired. Keeps nicely for weeks.

Dot Jerstad

Pink Salad

1 large can fruit cocktail (drained)
1 large can pineapple (chunks, tidbits or crushed, drained)
1 large carton cottage cheese
1 large carton Cool Whip
½ C. sugar
½ C. chopped nuts (optional)
½ package dry jello—strawberry or cherry flavor (you may use less if desired)

Mix together first 6 ingredients and sprinkle jello over and fold. Chill. Makes a large salad. Can be frozen.

Thelma Kemp

Vegetables

Vegetables

Spinach Casserole

2 small packages frozen spinach—
    chopped
1 small carton sour cream
1 package dry onion soup mix

Cook spinach according to the directions on package. Drain and cool. Mix soup mix and sour cream, add spinach. Cook in casserole dish in 300° oven for 20 minutes. Do not cover.

Judge Andrew T. "Tip" Taylor
Circuit Court Judge

Shoepeg Corn Casserole

½ C. chopped onion
⅓ C. green pepper
½ C. celery
1 C. French green beans—drained
1 C. shoepeg corn
1 C. celery soup
1 8 oz. sour cream
½ C. cheese—grated
Salt and pepper to taste
1 stack Ritz crackers
1 stick oleo—melted

Saute onion, green pepper, and celery. Add remaining ingredients except crackers and butter. Crumble crackers as a topping. Dribble melted butter over all. Bake at 350° for 30 minutes.

Nelda Jones

Baked Corn Casserole

1 can cream-style corn
1 12 oz. can whole kernel corn
½ C. grated onion
½ C. green pepper—chopped
2 pimentos—chopped
⅔ C. milk
1 egg—well beaten
1 C. grated American cheese
¼ C. melted butter
2 T. sugar
Black and Red pepper to taste
Salt to taste

Combine all ingredients, mix well. Pour into buttered 2 quart casserole. Bake at 350° for 1 hour. Makes 8 servings.

Camp Beans

4 cans beans
1 onion—chopped
1 bell pepper—chopped
½ C. white sugar
½ C. ketchup
1 t. hot sauce
1 t. black pepper
1 t. cayenne pepper

Mix all ingredients in large pan or dutch oven. Cook for 30–45 minutes on open fire, stove or in oven at 250°. Serves 8.

Rusty Schrivner

Asparagus Casserole

1 14 oz. can asparagus, cut spears
2 T. melted margarine
2 T. all purpose flour
½ C. shredded sharp cheddar
    cheese
½ C. slivered almonds
¾ C. buttered bread crumbs or
    cracker crumbs
Milk

Drain asparagus; reserve juice and add enough milk to make 1 C. Combine melted margarine and flour in sauce pan; cook until bubbly. Add reserved asparagus juice and milk and cook over medium heat, stirring constantly until sauce is medium thick. Layer asparagus, cheese, almonds, crumbs, and sauce in a 2-quart casserole dish. Repeat layers and top with buttered crumbs. Double sauce recipe if more asparagus is needed.

Sara T. Gowan

English Pea Casserole

1 sm. onion—chopped
1 green bell pepper—chopped
1 stick butter
2 cans English peas—drained
1 C. water chestnuts (with liquid)—
    chopped
1 can mushroom soup

Saute onion and pepper in butter. Add peas, water chestnuts, and mushroom soup. Put in square baking dish and top with buttered crumbs. Brown until bubbly and crumbs are brown.

Georgie Mallard

Spinach Casserole

2 packages frozen chopped
    spinach
2 eggs—beaten
2 onions—chopped (optional)
1 can Cream of Mushroom or
    chicken soup
1 C. grated cheddar cheese
½ C. mayonnaise

Boil, drain, and salt spinach. Combine with other ingredients. Top with cracker crumbs. Bake 45 minutes at 350°. Serve while hot.

Joyce Jones

Veg-All Casserole

2 cans Veg-All mixed vegetables—
   drained
1 C. onion—finely chopped
1 C. celery—finely chopped
1 C. grated cheese
1 C. mayonnaise
Salt and pepper
1 stack regular crackers—crushed
1 stick oleo—melted

Mix all ingredients; pour into greased casserole dish. Crush 1 stack regular crackers, mix with 1 stick melted oleo. Pour on top of other ingredients. Bake at 350° for 30–40 minutes. Serves 6.

Katharine Goodson

Vegetable Medley

1 10 oz. package each:
   Green beans
   Baby limas
   Whole kernel corn
   Carrots—diced or sliced
1 medium onion—chopped
2 T. oil
3 hard boiled eggs—chopped
2 T. Worcestershire sauce
Dash of Tobasco or hot sauce
¾ C. mayonnaise

Cook beans, limas, corn, and carrots until just tender. Then mix together. Keep real hot. Saute onion in oil, but do not brown. Add remaining ingredients to onion and pour over vegetables just before serving.

Dolly Mathis

Green Bean Casserole

2 cans French style green beans
½ C. chopped almonds
1 can cream of mushroom soup
8 oz. sour cream
1 C. grated cheddar cheese
1½ t. garlic salt
½ can French fried onions.

Butter casserole dish. Drain green beans and place in dish. Sprinkle almonds on beans. Combine mushroom soup, sour cream, and garlic salt. Layer this mixture on next. Sprinkle with cheese. Bake in 350° oven. After 30 minutes, sprinkle on French fried onions. Bake uncovered 15–30 minutes longer.

Tammy Hardee

Sweet and Sour Green Beans

2 cans green beans (French style)
6–8 strips bacon
1 small onion
¼–½ C. slivered almonds
6 T. sugar
6 T. vinegar
3 T. bacon drippings

Fry bacon until crisp, drain and crumble. Slice and separate the onion into rings. Drain green beans and add pepper and salt if needed. Layer beans, onion rings, almonds, and bacon in a casserole dish. Heat sugar, vinegar and bacon drippings in sauce pan until sugar is dissolved. Pour sauce over the vegetables and marinate overnight. Cook for 45 minutes at 350°.

Sara T. Gowan

Sweet and Sour Green Beans

2 cans French style green beans—
     drained
1 onion—sliced thin
8 slices bacon—fried crisp
Reserved bacon grease
6 T. dark vinegar
6 T. sugar

Layer green beans and onions in a casserole ending with a layer of beans. Fry bacon until crisp and set aside. Combine bacon when cool and put on top of mixture over beans. Marinate 6 to 8 hours. Bake in oven at 350° for 30 minutes. Sprinkle crumbled bacon over top. Serves 6.

Celia Willard Collins

Parmesan Potatoes

6 lg. potatoes
¼ C. sifted flour
¼ C. Parmesan Cheese
¾ t. salt
⅛ t. pepper
⅓ C. butter or oleo
Chopped parsley

Pare potatoes; cut into quarters. Combine flour, cheese, salt and pepper in a bag. Moisten potatoes with water and shake a few at a time in bag, coating potatoes well with cheese mixture. Melt butter in a 13 x 9 inch baking pan or dish. Place potatoes in a layer in pan. Bake at 375° for about 1 hour, turning once during baking. When golden brown, sprinkle with parsley.

Maurine Wilkins

Sweet Potato Casserole

1 lg. can sweet potatoes
½ stick margarine
½ t. apple pie spice
1½ C. sugar
3 eggs
¾ C. condensed milk
¾ C. potato juice
¼ t. vanilla

Heat potatoes and juice. Drain and save ¾ cup juice. Mash margarine with potatoes. Add apple pie spice, sugar, eggs, condensed milk, potato juice, and vanilla. Beat all together in mixer. Bake 1 hour at 350°. Put mixed topping on baked casserole. Place under broiler until brown.

June Childress

Topping:

3 T. flour
3 T. sugar
1½ t. apple pie spice
6 T. margarine
1½ C. chopped pecans

Sweet Potatoes with Apricots

1 large can sweet potatoes
½ C. brown sugar
¼ T. cornstarch
¼ t. salt
⅓ t. cinnamon
1 can apricot halves
1 T. butter—melted
1 C. chopped pecans

Mix sugar, cornstarch, salt and cinnamon. Drain apricots and save the syrup. Stir in one cup apricot juice and boil for 2 minutes. Cool and add apricots and pecans. Pour over sweet potatoes. Bake at 375° for 25 minutes.

Norma Taylor

Hash Brown Casserole

1 large bag hash browns—frozen
1 green pepper (chopped)
1 onion (chopped)
Salt, pepper to taste
2½ pints sour cream
1 can mushroom soup
1 can chicken soup

Mix thawed potatoes with other ingredients. Bake at 300° for 1 hour. Sprinkle top with grated cheese (cheddar or American) and buttered bread crumbs. Bake until brown.

Thelma Kemp

Sweet Potato Casserole

3 C. mashed sweet potatoes—
   cooked
½ C. sugar
2 eggs—beaten
½ t. salt
½ stick oleo—melted
½ C. milk
1½ t. vanilla

Topping:

½ C. brown sugar
⅓ C. flour
1 C. nuts—chopped
⅓ C. oleo—melted

Beat sugar, eggs, salt, oleo, milk and vanilla into mashed sweet potatoes. Add topping and bake at 350° for 30 minutes.

Joyce Jones

Sweet Potato Casserole

3 C. mashed sweet potatoes—
   cooked
1 C. sugar
2 eggs
1 T. vanilla
1 stick butter or oleo
1 can coconut

Topping:

1 C. brown sugar
½ C. flour
1 stick oleo—melted
1 C. chopped nuts

Mix all of the above ingredients together and put in casserole

Mix and spread on top of casserole. Bake uncovered until hot through and through and topping is melted and bubbly.

Imogene Tisdale

Family's Favorite Sweet Potato Casserole

3 medium-sized sweet potatoes
1 stick oleo
1 C. dark brown sugar
1 t. cinnamon
½ t. salt
½ t. nutmeg

Topping:

¼ stick oleo
½ C. sugar
2 T. milk
¼ t. salt
1 t. vanilla
½ C. pecan halves

Cook sweet potatoes in water; drain and mash. Place over low heat while adding sugar and oleo. Stir until melted and blended. Remove from heat. Add spices and salt and enough milk to make mashed potato consistency. Turn into greased baking dish. Cook the topping mixture over low heat stirring until thick and bubbly. Cool; add 1 t. vanilla and pour over potatoes. Sprinkle with ½ C. pecan halves on top. Bake at 350°–400° until thoroughly heated. Serve hot.

Susan Buntin Matthews

Squash Casserole

1½ C. squash—cooked (4–5 medium)
1 C. medium sharp cheese
1 small jar pimentos
2 eggs—well beaten
1 C. cracker crumbs
3 T. chopped onion
3 T. margarine—melted
1 C. milk—scalded
1½ t. salt
Pepper to taste

Combine all ingredients except milk—add last. Pour into greased baking dish. Bake one hour at 325°. Serves 6.

Annie Louise Dent

Broccoli and Rice Casserole

½ C. chopped onions
2 T. vegetable oil
1 package frozen, chopped broccoli
1 can cream of chicken soup
½ C. chopped celery
1 C. (uncooked) rice
1 can cream of mushroom soup
1 can cheddar cheese soup

Saute onion and celery in oil. Cook rice and broccoli separately. Combine other ingredients and bake in a 375° oven for 20 minutes.

Gloria Roberts

Squash Casserole

2 lbs. yellow squash
2 eggs
1 medium onion
1 t. pepper
1 can Cream of Mushroom soup
2 C. grated sharp cheese
3 or 4 slices of trimmed bread torn
in pieces

Cook squash in salted water until almost tender. Drain water. Place squash in casserole. Add remaining ingredients and mix. Bake at 325° for 1½ hours. Serves 6.

Diane Cathey

Deep South Okra and Tomatoes

1½ T. bacon drippings
4 C. sliced frozen okra
1 onion—finely chopped
1 t. salt
½ t. pepper
1 16 oz. can tomatoes

Melt drippings in skillet. Add okra and onion to drippings. Saute 5 minutes. Add salt, pepper, and tomatoes. Cover and simmer for 30 minutes stirring occasionally. Serves 6.

Sally Baker

Hoppin' John

½ lb. dry blackeyed peas
¼ C. chopped onion
1 small clove garlic—minced
1 T. oil
½ C. long grain white rice
½ C. cooked ham—cubed
½ t. salt
¼ t. pepper
¼ t. oregano
Dash crushed red chilli pepper
1 small bayleaf

Rinse peas; add 5 C. boiling water. Boil 2 minutes; remove from heat. Cover and soak 12 hrs. or overnight. (For a quick-soak method, add 5 C. boiling water to peas, boil 3 minutes, cover and let stand 1–4 hours). Drain and rinse peas. Saute onion and garlic in oil. Add soaked peas, rice, ham, 1½ C. water and seasonings; bring to boil. Reduce heat and simmer, covered, 25–30 minutes or until peas and rice are tender. Remove bay leaf.

Karen Hewitt Wimpee

Hopping John

1 C. dry black-eyed peas
¾ C. chopped onion
2 t. salt
8 C. water
1 clove minced garlic
¼ t. pepper
6 slices bacon
1 C. regular rice

Rinse black-eyed peas. In a large sauce pan, combine peas and water; bring to boil, boil for 2 minutes. Remove from heat and let stand 1 hour. Drain, reserving 6 cups of the liquid. In a heavy 3 quart saucepan, cook bacon, onion and garlic until bacon is crisp and onion is tender, but not brown. Remove bacon, drain on paper towels, crumble and set aside. Stir black-eyed peas, raw rice, salt, pepper, and the reserved liquid into mixture in saucepan. Bring to boil, cover, and reduce heat. Simmer 1 hour, stirring occasionally. Stir in crumbled bacon. Turn into a serving bowl. Serve immediately.

Jane Brackett

Potato Casserole

6 medium potatoes
2 C. shredded cheddar cheese
½ C. butter or margarine
2 C. sour cream—room
     temperature
½ C. chopped green onions
1 t. salt
½ t. white pepper
2 T. butter

Cook potatoes in skins. Cool and peel and coarsely shred. In sauce pan over low heat, combine cheese and butter. Stir until melted. Remove from heat and blend in sour cream, onions, salt, and pepper. Add potatoes, stir lightly. Turn into 2 quart casserole dish. Dot with butter and bake 25 minutes at 350°. Good served with steaks and other meats.

Joyce Jones

Chicken Stuffed Celery

1 3 oz. package cream cheese,
     softened
1 4 oz. can chicken spread
½ t. curry powder
24 pieces celery
Paprika

Combine mixture and chill. Spread on celery pieces. Serve cold.

Thelma Kemp

Vegetables

Cream of Potato Soup

3 lg. potatoes—diced
1 quart milk
½ C. chopped celery
1 T. butter
1 slice onion
1 T. salt
1 t. pepper
¼ C. chicken broth

Boil peeled potatoes 10 minutes. Drain. Put in fresh water, add broth, all the seasonings and cook until potatoes are tender. Put milk in double boiler and add flour and butter. When hot, stir until thick; pour into the potato mix and bring to boil.

Geni Holmes

Cheese Grits

4 C. boiling water
1 t. salt
1 C. quick cooking grits
6 oz. mild cheddar cheese—grated
1 stick margarine
2 T. milk
2 eggs—well beaten
Dash of garlic powder—optional

Bring water to boil, add salt and grits. Cook until thick. Remove from heat, add margarine and cheese. Stir until dissolved, add milk and eggs. Stir but do not beat; pour into greased casserole and bake at 400° for 45 minutes. Sprinkle with paprika before baking. Serves 10 people.

Joyce Jones

Spinach Lasagna

2 cloves garlic—minced
¼ lb. mushrooms—sliced
1 T. olive oil
2 T. melted oleo
2 15 oz. cans tomato sauce
1 T. chopped onion
2 T. minced parsley
½ t. salt
½ lb. lasagna noodles—cooked
    and drained
2 10 oz. packages frozen spinach
½ C. cottage cheese (small curd)
½ lb. mozzarella cheese—
    shredded
2 T. Parmesan cheese

Saute garlic and mushrooms in olive oil and butter. Add tomato sauce, onions, parsley, and salt. Simmer 10 minutes. Layer ½ noodles, spinach, cottage cheese, and mozzarella in greased pan. Pour ½ sauce over. Repeat. Sprinkle with parmesan. Serves 8–10.

Meats

Baked Chicken Oregano

1 chicken—cut up (Best of the
    fryer)
1 C. Regina cooking sherry
2 t. oregano—crumbled
Garlic salt to taste
Several small patties of butter
Pepper to taste
Minced onion bits to taste
Parsley—fresh chopped

Wash chicken thoroughly, trimming off excess fat. Place in baking pan, pour in sherry wine, season with butter, garlic salt, pepper, onion bits, and crumbled oregano on top. Bake for 1 hour at 350° in covered dish. Remove cover and broil for several minutes until golden brown.

Sandy and Wink Martindale

Sandy & Wink Martindale

Wink Martindale started his broadcasting career in his home town of Jackson, Tennessee, at the age of 16. Valuable on-air experience during the next two years at the three local Jackson stations, helped him land his first job at a major urban radio station. WHBQ in Memphis hired him as the "morning drive time" personality and combination record librarian.

In 1954, Wink was offered his first television job as host of a children's show titled "Wink Martindale of the Mars Patrol". A teen TV program followed in 1956, with Martindale hosting "Top Ten Dance Party".

1959 was a super year for Martindale. That year he moved his radio and television career to Los Angeles, recorded a million-seller record and album, "Deck of Cards", and performed the narrative on the "Ed Sullivan Show".

In 1965, Martindale auditioned for and won the host job on his first NBC game show, "What's This Song?" He went on to host a number of other game shows, such as "Can You Top This", "Dream Girl '67", "Gambit", and the highly successful and popular, "Tic-Tac-Dough". Even with his demanding schedule Martindale hosts a daily drive-time radio show afternoons on Gene Autry's 50 thousand watt flagship station in Los Angeles, KMPC.

Wink got his nickname as a boy growing up in Jackson, Tennessee. Winston C. Martindale was too much of a mouthful for a 5-year-old neighborhood playmate, so the chum called him "Winky". Sometime during adolescence, the nickname, which obviously stuck, lost its "y".

Martindale is the father of four grown children. He and his wife, Sandy, with their 10-year-old silkie dog, "Gambit", live in a newly purchased home in Malibu, California.

Chicken Deluxe

1 C. flour
3 t. salt
¼ t. pepper
2 t. paprika
6 chicken breast halves
¼ C. butter or margarine
¼ C. cooking oil
3 C. celery—chopped
1 can cream of chicken soup
½ C. Half & Half
2 T. pimento—chopped
1 C. American cheese—grated
1 C. bread crumbs
2 T. butter—melted
½ C. slivered almonds

Combine flour, salt, pepper and paprika. Roll chicken breasts in mixture and brown in the butter and oil. Place celery in the bottom of a greased, 3-quart casserole dish. Place chicken breasts on top of celery. Combine soup, cream, pimento, and cheese and pour over the chicken. Top with buttered bread crumbs and almonds. Bake 45 minutes at 350°. May be prepared ahead and stored in the refrigerator. Allow to reach room temperature before cooking.

Annie Louise Dent

Pauletde Normandise Chicken Casserole

1 package seasoned Pepperidge
　Farm bread stuffing (not
　cornbread)
1 stick melted oleo
1 C. water
2½ C. cooked chicken breast—cut
　up fine
½ C. chopped onion
½ C. chopped celery
½ C. mayonnaise
¾ t. salt
2 eggs
1½ C. milk
1 can Cream of Mushroom soup
¾ C. grated cheese

Mix stuffing, oleo, and water. Put half this mixture in bottom of 12 x 9 buttered casserole dish. Separately mix chicken, onion, celery, mayonnaise, and salt. Place this over bread mixture in dish. Put other half of bread mixture on top of this and press in well. Beat eggs, add milk. Pour this over top of casserole. Cover with foil and refrigerate overnight. Take out of refrigerator 1 hour before baking. Spread 1 can Cream of Mushroom soup over top. Bake uncovered at 325° for 40 minutes. Return with grated cheese on top and bake another 10 minutes. Serves 12.

Serena Mitchell

Three-Cheese Chicken Bake

8 oz. Lasagna noodles
½ C. chopped onion
½ C. chopped green pepper
3 T. butter or margarine
1 can condensed Cream of Chicken soup
1 6 oz. can sliced mushrooms—drained
½ C. chopped pimento—drained
⅓ C. milk
½ t. dried basil, crushed
1½ C. cream-style cottage cheese
2 C. diced cooked chicken
2 C. shredded American cheese
½ C. grated Parmesan cheese

Cook noodles in boiling salted water according to package directions; drain. Cook onion and pepper in butter or margarine until tender. Stir in soup, mushrooms, pimento, milk, and basil. Lay half the noodles in a 13 x 9 x 2 baking dish; top with half each of the sauce, cottage cheese, chicken and American and Parmesan cheese. Repeat layers except for last two cheeses. Bake 45 minutes at 350°. Top with cheeses, bake 2 minutes more. Serves 8–10.

Dot Exum

Poppy Seed Chicken

6 chicken breasts
1 large container sour cream
1 can Cream of Chicken soup
2 T. poppy seed
1 roll crushed Ritz crackers
1½ sticks melted butter

Boil and debone chicken. Mix chicken, soup, sour cream and poppy seeds; place in long pyrex dish. Combine crackers and butter and spread over top. Cover and bake at 350° for 30 minutes. Serves 6 to 8.

Deborah Shaw Laman

Parmesan Chicken Breasts

½ C. butter—melted
1 C. Parmesan cheese
1½–2 C. bread crumbs
8 chicken breasts—deboned
Garlic salt
Fresh parsley

Dip breasts in melted butter. Roll in mixture of cheese, bread crumbs, and garlic salt. Top with parsley in uncovered glass baking dish. Pour unused butter over top of breasts. Bake 1½ hours at 350°. When done, accent with parsley sprigs. Serves 6–8.

Maurine Wilkins

Chicken Broccoli

1 chicken
1 package frozen chopped broccoli
1 can Cream of Chicken soup
1 C. rice—cooked in chicken broth
1 can water chestnuts—sliced
1 small jar Cheez Whiz

Stew chicken, remove from broth, and debone, chop. Cook rice in broth. Put broccoli in with rice toward end of cooking time. Stir all ingredients together. Top with Cheese Whiz and bake at 350° about 20 minutes.

Bonnie Cummings

Chicken and Stuffing Casserole

4 chicken breasts—cooked and chopped
Small package Pepperidge Farm stuffing (herb)
Small carton sour cream
1 can cream of chicken soup
1 stick oleo—melted

Mix oleo, stuffing mix, soup, sour cream, and some broth. Put ½ the mixture in bottom of greased casserole dish. Place chicken in the middle and rest of mixture on top. Bake at 350° until lightly browned (about 30 minutes). May substitute 8 chicken thighs and Chicken flavor Stove Top Stuffing.

Elizabeth Harris

Mexican Chicken

4 large chicken breasts (fillets)
2 cans Cream of Chicken soup
1 can Rotel (chopped) tomatoes
1 C. chopped bell peppers
1 C. chopped onion
½ T. garlic powder
½ T. chili powder
1 C. grated sharp cheddar cheese
1 large bag regular flavor Doritos

Boil chicken. Cut into small pieces. Mix together soup, Rotel, bell peppers, onion, garlic, chili powder, and ½ cup of cheese. Spray a large pyrex pan with Pam. Line bottom with ½ cup of crushed Doritos. Place chicken pieces on top. Pour in mixed ingredients. Bake at 350° for 30 minutes. Pour remaining Doritos and cheese over top and return to oven until cheese melts. (Tip -, when crushing Doritos, cut the corner off to release air and mash with hand.)

Joyce Laman Millard

Dressing for Turkey or chicken

1 apple—finely chopped
1 orange—finely chopped
1 large can crushed pineapple
1 lemon rind—grated
1 C. drained water chestnuts—
   chopped
2 t. mild mustard
1 T. oregano
1 bay leaf—well crushed
1 t. black pepper
4 T. parsley—chopped
4 garlic cloves—mashed
4 cloves—mashed
3 large onions—chopped
6 stalks celery—chopped
1 T. poultry seasoning
Bread crumbs from 6 biscuits
Bread crumbs from cornbread
1 lb. sausage—cooked and drained
¼ lb. butter or margarine—melted

In one bowl mix apple, orange, pineapple, lemon rind, and water chestnuts. In second bowl mix mustard, oregano, bay leaf, pepper, parsley, garlic, cloves, onions, celery, and poultry seasoning. In third bowl mix bread crumbs, sausage, and butter. Then mix contents of all three bowls together, mix well. Add stock from giblets. If mixture is not moist enough, add some canned chicken broth. Turkey can be stuffed with some of this dressing and the rest cooked separately.

Jane Parham for
City Commissioner Johnny Parham

Country Cordon

4 boneless chicken breasts
4 slices Mozarella cheese
4 slices bacon—partly cooked
3 T. vegetable oil
2 cans condensed cream of
   chicken soup
Salt, pepper, & parsley to taste

Using a mallet, pound chicken breast until about ⅛ inch thick. Salt, pepper, and parsley to taste. Place 1 slice cheese and 1 slice bacon on top of chicken. Roll up jelly-roll style and secure with toothpick. Brown chicken roll-ups in oil on both sides till golden brown. Thin the cream of chicken soup with milk; pour over chicken. Bring to a boil over medium heat; then simmer, covered, for 25 minutes.

Juanita Shaw

Pineapple Chicken

4 lbs. chicken—cut up
½ t. salt
¼ t. celery salt
¼ t. nutmeg
2 T. soy sauce
¼ t. garlic
½ C. butter or oleo
20 oz. can crushed pineapple
3–4 C. cooked rice

Wash and dry chicken. Stir 4 seasonings together, rub into chicken. Melt oleo in 13 x 9 baking dish. Place chicken skin side down in dish. Bake uncovered 30 minutes at 425°. Turn chicken. Drain pineapple and reserve juice. Mix juice and soy sauce and pour over chicken. Bake another 15 minutes. Spoon pineapple over chicken pieces and reheat 10 minutes. Serve with rice.

Mildred H. Couch

Chicken Loaf

3 C. cooked chicken—cubed
½ C. chicken broth
1 C. cooked rice
1½ C. bread crumbs (seasoned croutons)
¾ C. milk
2 T. pimento—chopped
4 eggs—beaten

Combine all ingredients in order given. Put in loaf pan. Bake at 350° for 45 minutes. Serve with or without sauce.

Sauce:

4 T. margarine
1 C. milk
4 T. flour
1 small can mushrooms
¼ C. chopped parsley

Mix margarine, flour, and milk over heat until desired consistency. Add small can mushrooms and chopped parsley. Serve hot

Dolly Mathis

Chicken and Rice Casserole

3 C. chicken or turkey—cooked and
    chopped
1 box Uncle Ben Wild Rice
1 medium onion—chopped
1 can French-style green beans—
    drained
1 can water chestnuts—sliced and
    drained
1 medium jar pimentos—drained
    and diced
1 can celery soup
1 C. Helman's mayonnaise
Salt and pepper to taste

Cook rice and add to other ingredients. Bake at 350° for 30–35 minutes. May freeze (do not bake until ready to eat).

Dorothy Sue Goodrich

Creamed Chicken
(To use over Spoon Bread)

½ c. chopped celery
¼ C. butter or oleo
⅓ C. flour
Salt to taste
1 13 oz. can condensed chicken
    broth
2 C. cooked chicken—cubed
2 T. canned pimento—chopped
Parsley

Cook celery in butter until tender but not browned. Blend in flour. Stir in the condensed chicken broth. Cook and stir until thickened and bubbly. Add chicken, chopped pimento, and salt. Heat through. To serve, ladle creamed chicken mixture over portions of hot spoon bread. Garnish with parsley if desired.

Pauline (Polly) Long

Deluxe Country Fried Chicken

1 large cut-up chicken
1 egg
1½ C. milk
2 C. flour
Salt and pepper to taste

Beat egg and milk together. Roll salted chicken in flour, dip in milk and egg mixture, then roll in flour again. Fry in deep-fat fryer until pieces float to top and are golden brown.

Shirley Droke

Bradford's Doodle Soup and Chicken

1 baking hen
10–12 c. broth
1½ C. vinegar—to taste
Red ceyenne pepper—to taste
2 T. flour
6 livers—cooked and chopped
6 gizzards—cooked and chopped
12 eggs—hard boiled

Cook hen in roaster, almost covered with water, in a 350° oven for 2½ hours. When done, measure 10–12 cups broth into Dutch oven. Add flour, vinegar and pepper and boil for 20–30 minutes; simmer for at least an hour. Cut up cooked livers, gizzards and hard-boiled eggs and combine together, spoon onto crumbled crackers or hot biscuits which have been placed in individual serving dishes. Pour soup over all. Serve deboned chicken on side. Cream potatoes, English peas, and fruit salad should always be served with Doodle Soup and Chicken.

Minestrone Soup

12 oz. hamburger
8 C. water
4 beef bouillon cubes
1 C. chopped onion
2 C. chopped cabbage
2 C. diced carrots
2 C. diced zucchini
2 C. canned tomatoes
2 C. kidney beans
1 clove garlic
½ t. pepper
1 t. crushed oregano
¼ C. chopped parsley
1 C. raw macaroni

Brown meat, drain fat, add water and bouillon, add onion, cabbage and carrots. Bring to a boil and simmer 30 minutes. Add remaining and simmer until macaroni is cooked.

Margaret Hewitt

Lazy Man's Quick Spaghetti
(Basgetti: All Kids Love It)

1 lb. ground chuck
1 can tomato sauce
Celery salt
3 medium size onions—diced
2 large cans Franco American
**   Spaghetti**
Parmesan cheese (optional)

Grease iron skillet with just enough shortening to cover bottom. Add diced onions, cook over medium low heat until tender. Mix in ground chuck. Cook slowly until meat is done (5–10 minutes). Add tomato sauce, Franco American Spaghetti, and sprinkle with celery salt. Simmer low for 5–10 minutes. Salt and sprinkle Parmesan cheese to suit individual taste; and ENJOY, ENJOY. Serves 6. This freezes well, and is actually better the second day after refrigeration all night.

Doris "Cousin Tuny" Freeman

Doris "Cousin Tuny" Freeman

Doris "Cousin Tuny" Freeman, mother of four children and grandmother of four, is in much demand for speaking, emceeing and entertaining, and has earned respect for many years as a successful professional business woman.

She began her career at the age of 7, singing and dancing on radio. She was featured singer and entertainer with the Moonglows Dance Combo for many years. She created and starred in a daily "Cousin Tuny" children's TV show for twelve years. During these years, she also worked in radio programming and on the air including broadcasting the Miss Tennessee Pageant, also covering the Miss America Pageant from Press Row in Atlantic City for many years, and was Top Radio Advertising Executive for the Mid-South area, serving as Sales Manager of a radio station. She blended in a promotional and advertising free lance business during these years that included Manager and Marketing Director of Old Hickory Mall in Jackson. She is presently Director of Marketing and Public Relations for Jackson Madison County General Hospital. Beautifully balanced against her career, however, have been the tasks of a single mother raising her four children plus her many and varied services to charity, religious, and civic organizations. She has received numerous honors throughout her career.

She was the First Woman Ambassador for Jackson Area Chamber of Commerce, and is an active member of the First United Methodist Church of Jackson, Tennessee.

Railroad Pie

1 lb. ground beef
1 onion—chopped
1 can tomato soup
1 C. water
1 t. salt
1 T. chili powder
1 C. whole kernel corn

Topping:

¾ C. plain meal
¾ t. sugar
1 t. salt
1 T. flour
¼ t. soda
1 egg
½ C. buttermilk

Brown ground beef and onion together. Add other ingredients and simmer 15 minutes. Place in 1½ quart casserole dish. Spoon topping over top and bake 30–40 minutes at 350°.

Joyce Jones

Johnny Morzetti

1 lb. ground beef
3 large onions
4 ribs celery
1 green pepper
1 small can mushrooms
1 can Chef Boy-Ar-Dee spaghetti
    sauce with mushrooms
1 can tomato soup
1 medium can tomato juice
1 t. sugar
½ jar olives
½ lb. grated sharp cheese
1 package fine noodles
1 stick oleo

Brown meat in oleo, onions, pepper, celery, and mushrooms. Add sauce, soup, juice, sugar, olives, and cheese. Mix with pre-cooked noodles. Bake 1 hour at 350°.

Kelley Walker

Barbecued Meat Balls

1½ lbs. ground beef
2 t. salt
½ C. milk
¼ t. pepper
1 C. catsup
¼ C. Worcestershire sauce
3 T. onion—chopped
1 t. sugar
2 t. vinegar
1 T. water

Mix together ground beef, salt, milk, and pepper and shape in 16 balls. Fry in small amount of fat until browned. Mix remaining ingredients and pour over meat in skillet. Cover and cook slowly 30 minutes, turning meat occasionally. Serves 4 to 6.

Maurine Wilkins

Hamburger Stroganoff

1 lb. ground beef
½ onion—chopped
1 can mushroom soup
1 carton sour cream
Salt and pepper to taste

Brown beef and onion. Pour off fat and add seasonings. Stir in mushroom soup; simmer 5 minutes. Stir in sour cream. Serve over cooked rice. Serves 4.

Katharine Goodson

Ranch-Style Hash

1–1½ lbs. ground beef
1 large can pork and beans
1–2 C. sharp cheddar cheese—cut
   into pieces

Add all ingredients to browned and drained ground beef in a large iron skillet. Cook on a medium burner until thickens and cheese has melted. Serve over toast. 6–8 servings.

Lucile O. Johnson

Ground Beef Casserole

1 large potato—sliced
1 medium onion—sliced
1 large carrot—sliced
¼ cabbage—chopped fine
1 lb. ground beef
1 can Cream of Tomato Soup
1 C. water

Layer the first five ingredients as listed. Pour water, then tomato soup over all. Bake at 350° for 1½ hours. Good served with corn bread.

Virginia L. Sculley

Meatloaf

2 lbs. ground beef
1 envelope onion soup mix
2 eggs
¼ C. ketchup
¼ C. barbecue sauce
1½ C. soft bread crumbs
¾ C. evaporated milk

Preheat oven to 350°. In large bowl, combine meatloaf ingredients and mix well. Shape into loaf and place in baking dish. Cover and bake 45 minutes to 1 hour.

Topping:

1 C. firmly packed brown sugar,
    preferably dark
¼ t. ground mustard
Ketchup
Barbecue sauce

Mix sugar and mustard with just enough ketchup and barbecue sauce to spread well. It should be thick. Place on top of meatloaf 10 minutes before final baking time and finish baking uncovered.

Rebecca B. Porter

Lasagna

2 lbs. hamburger
1 onion—chopped
1 12 oz. can tomato paste
1 lb. can tomatoes
1 C. water
1 t. oregano
1 t. sweet basil
⅛ t. garlic powder
1½ t. salt
10 oz. lasagna noodles

Brown hamburger and onion and drain. Add remaining ingredients and simmer for 30 minutes or until thick. Cook noddles in large amount of boiling water. Drain.

24 oz. cottage cheese
½ C. Parmesan cheese
2 T. dried parsley
2 eggs—beaten
1½ t. salt
½ t. pepper
6 oz. Mozzarella cheese—for
    topping

Mix together cheeses, parsley, eggs, salt, and pepper. Place half the noodles in 13 x 9 x 2 baking dish; spread with half of the cottage cheese filling; add half of the meat sauce. Repeat layers. Top with thin sliced or grated Mozarella cheese. Bake at 375° 30 minutes. Can assemble early and refrigerate. Allow 15 minutes longer in oven. Let stand 10 minutes before cutting.

Nelda Rhodes

Baked Spaghetti

1 lb. ground beef
½ C. onion—chopped
½ t. salt
1 large can Franco American
    Spaghetti and Tomato Sauce
1 jar Kraft pimento cheese spread

Brown beef and onions. Add seasoning; stir in can of spaghetti and tomato sauce. Add jar of cheese spread. Mix and pour in a large casserole dish. Bake at 350° for 30 minutes. Serves 6.

Katharine Goodson

Mexican Delight

1 lb. ground beef
2 cans chili without beans
1 can cheddar cheese soup
1 box minute rice
Lettuce
Cheese
Tomatoes
Fritos Corn Chips

Brown ground beef, add chili and cheddar cheese soup. Simmer 30 minutes, then put over prepared rice. Top with cheese, lettuce tomatoes, and corn chips.

Peggy Haywood

Spanish Rice with Beef

1 medium onion—finely chopped
1 medium green pepper—chopped
2 lbs. ground beef
2 C. uncooked rice
2 C. hot water
1½ t. salt
1 t. mustard
½ C. cheddar cheese—grated

In heavy skillet, lightly brown onion, ground beef, green pepper, and rice. Add remaining ingredients, mix well. Bring to boil; cover and simmer 25 minutes. Remove to pyrex dish, sprinkle with grated cheese. Place in hot oven until cheese melts. This recipe halved makes good stuffing for green peppers.

Mrs. Charles E. Hall

Spanish Rice

½ lb. bacon—cut up
½ lb. hamburger
1 medium onion—chopped
2 C. water
1 C. uncooked rice
⅛ teaspoon pepper
⅔ C. chopped green pepper
1 16 oz. can tomatoes
1 t. oregano
1¼ t. salt
1 t. chili powder

Cook bacon, hamburger, and onion together; drain. Stir in remaining ingredients. Heat to boiling; reduce heat. Cover and simmer, stirring occasionally until rice is tender, about 30 minutes.

Judy Martin

Chili

2 lb. ground beef
3 cans (16 oz.) Chili Hot beans
1 can (10 oz.) tomato soup
1 can (8 oz.) tomato sauce
1 chopped onion
1½ T. chili powder
¼ t. red pepper
¼ t. black pepper
½ t. ground cumin
1 T. salt
¼ t. oregano
1 T. sugar

Brown ground beef and onion in large pan. Add spices. Mix well. Add chili beans, soup, and tomato sauce. Add more spices and salt as needed. Simmer for 45 minutes.

Geni Holmes

Chili

1 lb. ground beef
½ onion—chopped
1 package chili mix
1 can tomato soup
1 can water

Brown ground beef and onion. Add chili mix, soup and water. Simmer 30 minutes and serve with Fritos corn chips.

Katharine Goodson

Chili

1 large onion—chopped
1 can whole tomatoes
1 large can tomato sauce
2 T. Worcestershire sauce
1½ t. chili powder
1 T. garlic powder
2 cans pinto beans
1 lb. ground beef—cooked and
  drained

Combine ingredients, salt and pepper to taste. Cook in slow cooker for 3 hours.

Mary Garrett

Beef Stroganoff

1 lb. ground beef
1 chopped onion
1 t. salt
1 8 oz. sour cream
1 can mushrooms
1 can Cream of Mushroom soup
½ t. pepper
1 small package noodles—cooked

Brown onion and ground beef. Add salt and pepper, soup and mushrooms. Cook over low heat for 45 minutes. Add sour cream and serve over cooked noodles.

Geni Holmes

Fried Rice and Meat

1 medium onion—chopped
2 T. oil
½ lb. ground beef
4 C. cooked rice—cooled
2 T. soy sauce
1 egg—beaten
1 t. salt
½ t. black pepper

Put oil in pan, heat. Add onion and meat. Cook and stir over medium heat until onion is tender. Add rice, soy sauce, ½ t. salt, ½ t. black pepper. Stir egg into rice mixture. Cook and stir 5 minutes. Makes 4 servings.

Dorothy Mitchell

Country Steaks & Gravy

2 lb. ground beef
4 egg yolks
1 C. chopped onion

Gravy:

1 can Cream of Mushroom soup
1 package dried onion soup mix
8 C. water

Mix ingredients and form patties. Brown in iron skillet until done, turning once. Place in baking dish.

Mix ingredients and pour ½ over steaks and bake at 350° for 30 minutes. Serves 12 to 15.

Cynthia Grimsley

Sunday Roast and Gravy

1 medium-sized roast
1 can Cream of Mushroom soup
1 package dried onion soup mix
1 C. water
3–4 fresh carrots or 1 package
    sliced frozen carrots
3 or 4 whole potatoes—quartered

Place roast in 9 x 13 pan and salt. Add remaining ingredients on top of meat, arranging vegetables around it. Cover *tightly* with aluminum foil. Bake at 325° about 3 hours. Ready to eat when you get home from church. Makes it own rich gravy which is delicious over rice or creamed potatoes.

Shirley Droke

Preacher's Pepper Steak

1 round steak
1 green bell pepper
1 medium onion
1 C. water
¼ C. oil
Flour

Cut steak into small pieces. Salt and roll in flour. Lightly brown both sides in ¼ C. oil in electric skillet. Add cut-up pepper and onion. Pour in water and simmer, covered, for 30 to 45 minutes. Delicious served over rice.

Shirley Droke

Zip 'n' Dash Rice and Steak Bake

1 stick margarine
1 onion—chopped
1 bell pepper—chopped
½–1 lb. round steak
1 C. rice
2 cans beef broth or boullion

Cut steak into thin strips. Melt a stick of margarine in a skillet and in it brown onion, pepper, and steak strips. In a 2-quart casserole, combine meat, peppers, onions, and margarine with one cup rice (NOT minute rice). Pour beef broth or boullion over the mixture, and bake in a 300° oven for an hour. Serves two generously.

Delores Ballard

Green Noodle Casserole

1 12 oz. package spinach noodles
1 whole chicken
1 C. celery—finely chopped
1 C. onion—finely chopped
1 C. bell pepper—finely chopped
1 stick butter
1 can cream of mushroom soup
1 can cream of chicken soup
1 lb. Velveeta Cheese—cubed
1 large can mushrooms—chopped
Slivered almonds

Boil chicken in 2 quarts water. Saute vegetables in butter. Add soups (undiluted) and cheese. Cut chicken into bite-sized pieces and add it and mushrooms to mixture. Skim fat from chicken stock and cook noddles just until tender and most of stock is absorbed. Mix in noodles. Put in large casserole. Sprinkle top with slivered almonds. Cook at 350° for 45 minutes. Do not use another kind of noodles. Serves 10–12.

Becky Locke

Oven Pork Chops

4 pork chops
½ C. tomato catsup
1 6 oz. Coke or 7-up
Salt and pepper

Salt and pepper to taste. Put chops in baking dish. Mix ½ C. catsup and ½ Coca-Cola or 7-up. Pour over chops— then pour remaining Coke or 7-up over chops. Bake in a 350° oven for about 1 hour or until sauce is cooked up.

Thelma Kemp

East Union Stew

2½ lbs. beef roast
1 chicken
3 large onions
4 large potatoes
2 16 oz cans tomatoes
2 16 oz. cans mixed vegetables
1 pod red pepper
1 16 oz. can tomato puree
1½ stick oleo
2 T. Crisco
2 16 oz. cans cream corn
Salt & pepper to taste
Ketchup to taste

Cook beef roast 1 hour, add chicken to roast and cook 1½ hours more; remove bones. Cook vegetables until tender, add corn to stew about 30 minutes before stew is done. Stir and boil at low temperature. If cooked too much, add some tomato ketchup.

John Andrew Hawk

Meaty Spare Ribs

4 or 5 lbs. Country style ribs
½ C. vinegar
½ C. sugar
½ C. brown sugar
1 T. flour
1 C. water
½ C. catsup
1 t. soy sauce
1 can (15 oz.) pineapple tidbits

Cover ribs with water. Add salt and pepper and boil until real tender; then drain and place in large pan. Combine smoothly all other ingredients and pour over ribs. Bake 1 hour at 325°. Baste frequently. Serves 8.

Wanda Fowler

Pork Chop Casserole

4–6 pork chops
8–10 medium potatoes
1 can cream of mushroom soup or
    cream of chicken soup
1 medium onion
Salt & pepper
1 quart of milk

Thinly slice potatoes into large baking dish. Add minced onion. Heat soup in separate pan and pour over potatoes. Lay chops on top of potatoes. Add salt and pepper to taste. Pour milk over all until it reaches about 1 inch from top of pan. Cover with foil and bake 1 hour at 350°. Uncover and bake about 30 minutes more. Can add vegetables if desired.

Baked Pork Chops

Desired number of pork chops
Butter
Pepper
Garlic salt
Worcestershire sauce

Place desired number of pork chops in 9 x 13 baking dish. Put butter on each pork chop, then sprinkle with pepper and garlic salt. Pour Worcestershire sauce on top. Bake 1 hour at 375°.

Diane Crouch

Sausage and Wild Rice Casserole

1 lb. sausage—crumble and brown
1 can water chestnuts—chopped
½ C. celery—chopped
1 small onion—chopped
2 packages of Lipton Chicken
    Noodle Soup Mix
1 box Uncle Ben's Long Grain Rice
    (6 oz.)
1 small can mushrooms
4½ C. water

Combine ingredients in order given. Bake in casserole at 325° for 1-1½ hours. If casserole becomes dry, add a little more water.

Sharon Deaton

Frozen Ham Sandwiches

2 sticks margarine—melted
3 T. prepared mustard
1 small onion—grated (optional)
1½ T. poppy seeds
1 T. Worcestershire sauce
Sesame buns
Ham—shaved
Swiss cheese slices

Mix margarine, mustard, onion, poppy seeds, and Worcestershire sauce and refrigerate. Cover tops and bottoms of buns with mixture. Add ham and cheese. Wrap in foil and freeze. Bake at 350° for 30 minutes. Serves 8–10 people.

Leigh Ann Jones

Sweet and Sour Pork

Cooking oil
1 egg
¼ C. flour
1 t. salt
Dash of pepper
3 T. milk
1 lb. lean pork (cut in 1″ cubes)
1 C. pineapple chunks
⅓ C. vinegar
1 large green pepper—chopped
½ C. brown sugar
1 chicken bouillon cube
1 C. boiling water
2 t. soy sauce
2 T. cornstarch
1 tomato (cut in 6 pieces)

Heat oil to 350° F. Mix egg, flour, salt, pepper and milk to make a thin batter. Dip pork in batter and fry in deep oil until golden brown. Dissolve bouillon cube in 1 C. boiling water. Combine pineapple, vinegar, green pepper, brown sugar, ¾ C. chicken bouillon and soy sauce. Bring to a boil. Mix cornstarch and remaining ¼ C. bouillon and stir into sauce. Cook until thickened. Fold in tomato and pork. Cook about 2 minutes more. Serve immediately with hot cooked rice. Serves 6.

Karen Hewitt Wimpee

Ham and Cheese Souffle

16 slices day old bread
16 slices ham (⅛″ thick)
16 slices Swiss and American
 cheese
6 eggs
3 C. milk
½ t. onion salt
2 C. crushed corn flake crumbs
½ C. oleo—melted

Trim crust from bread. Grease 9 x 13 pan. Layer bread, ham, cheese, bread, ham, cheese. Beat eggs with milk and salt and pour over layers. Cover and refrigerate overnight. Melt oleo and mix with corn flake crumbs and spread over the top. Preheat oven to 400° and bake 40 minutes; serve immediately. Makes 8–12 servings.

Imogene Tisdale

Sour Cream Chicken Breasts

6 chicken breasts
1 can mushroom soup
1 can mushrooms or ½ C. fresh
1 C. sour cream
Hot cooked rice

Put chicken in 9 x 13 inch Pyrex dish. Mix soup, mushrooms, and sour cream. Pour over chicken. Bake, uncovered, in a 325° oven for 1½ hours. Serve over rice.

Juanita Shaw

Sausage Pie

1 unbake pie shell
½ lb. mild sausage
3 eggs—beaten
1 C. sour cream
1 t. Worcestershire
½ t. salt
1 C. grated cheese

Fry sausage to just brown and drain. Add eggs, sour cream, worcestershire, salt and cheese. Bake 10 minutes at 425° and reduce heat to 350° and bake for 30 minutes or until knife comes out clean.

Mary Kathryn Crowley

Pizza by the Foot

1 loaf French bread
1 6 oz. can tomato paste
⅓ C. grated Parmesan cheese
¼ C. chopped ripe olives
¼ C. chopped onion
½ t. oregano
½ t. salt
1 lb. ground beef
2 sliced tomatoes
4 oz. shredded American cheese

Cut bread in half lengthwise. Combine tomato paste, parmesan cheese, onion, olives, oregano, salt and pepper. Add browned ground beef, mix well. Spread on loaf halves. Place on baking sheet. Bake at 400° for 20 minutes. Remove from oven, top with tomato slices, and sprinkle cheese on top. Serves 4.

Geni Holmes

Seafood Casserole

1 lb. fresh shrimp
1 to 2 cans crab meat
1 cup celery, chopped
1 green pepper, chopped
1 medium onion, chopped
1 cup mayonnaise
1 cup water chestnuts, sliced
1 to 2 jars of mushrooms, sliced
    or 1 package fresh mushrooms,
    sautéed
1 tablespoon Worcestershire
1 tablespoon chopped parsley
1 tablespoon fresh lemon juice
Salt to taste
White pepper to taste
1 cup herb dressing mix (like
    Pepperidge Farm) (Save ⅓
    dressing mix for topping)

Mix all ingredients. Put in 9 x 13 casserole dish. Bake at 350° for 20 to 30 minutes. Serves 10–12.

Joyce Smith
Jackson, Tennessee

Shrimp Gumbo

1 tall can tomato juice or 1 large
   can tomatoes—well chopped
½ C. bell pepper—finely chopped
3 medium onions
1 clove garlic
1 T. chili powder
1 bay leaf
Salt & pepper to taste
3 T. bacon grease
3 T. flour
3 lbs. shrimp
2 T. shrimp boil
2 C. rice—cooked
2–3 C. okra

Combine tomatoes and bell peppers. Saute onions and garlic in bacon grease. Add chili powder, bay leaf, salt and pepper. Lightly brown flour in bacon grease; add water to make right consistency. Add to tomato mixture. Cook, peel, and devein shrimp in boiling water with 2 T. shrimp boil. Add with rice to tomato mixture. Stir well. Serves 12.

Jane Parham
For Commissioner Johnny Parham

Johnny Parham

    When asked to submit recipes for the OLD COUNTRY STORE COOKBOOK, Johnny asked his wife, Jane, to assist, as she does the cooking in their family.

    Johnny and Jane (Harris) were both born and raised in Jackson. They married in 1937 and have five children and seven grandchildren. The Parhams, all of their children, and all but one of their grandchildren live in Jackson.

    Johnny Parham served ten years on the Madison County Court, beginning in 1966, until 1977. At that time, he was elected City Commissioner and has served in this capacity for the past nine years.

    He and Jane have both been active in church, civic, and community affairs, and enjoy good cooking, good eating, and good friends.

Seafood Gumbo

1½ to 2 lbs shrimp
1 to 2 cans claw crab meat
4 T. shortening
4 T. flour
1 or 2 cloves garlic—minced
Cayenne—to taste
1 large onion—chopped
1 bell pepper—chopped
1 C. celery—chopped
1 can stewed tomatoes
1 can water
2 C. okra—chopped

Saute onion, pepper, and celery in shortening; add okra, tomatoes, and garlic; add salt, pepper, and cayenne to taste and let simmer until okra is about tender. Thicken with flour by using a little of the moisture; add 1½ to 2 lbs. shrimp and one to two cans of claw crab meat (or a combination of crab, shrimp, and oysters) simmer about 20 minutes more. Makes about ½ gallon. Is good served over rice or as a soup. Is best if made ahead and let to set a while before serving.

Dollie Mathis

Tuna Noodle Casserole

1 7 oz. can tuna
3 C. medium white sauce
8 oz. noodles
Buttered bread crumbs

Drain and flake tuna. Add to white sauce and heat. Layer cooked noodles and cream tuna in a buttered casserole. Sprinkle bread crumbs on top. Bake in 350° oven for 20 minutes.

White sauce:

¼ C. Crisco
¼ C. flour
2 C. milk
1 t. salt

Melt Crisco in saucepan. Stir in flour. Add milk and salt. Cook and stir over low heat until thickened. Makes 2 cups.

Geni Holmes

Salmon Loaf

1 lb. pink salmon—drained
2 eggs—beaten
1 can undiluted celery soup
½ C. onions—chopped
1 C. bread crumbs
1 t. lemon juice

Mix all ingredients together. Put in greased loaf pan. Bake at 375° for 1 hour. Makes 6 servings.

Dorothy Mitchell

Fried Pink Salmon

1 can pink salmon
2 T. flour
½ C. corn meal
1 egg
⅓ C. milk

Remove large bones from salmon. Mix all ingredients together, mix well. Fry in hot vegetable oil or lard.

Evora Summars

Blackstone Eggs
(from the famous Chicago hotel)

4 beefsteak tomatoes
10 strips of bacon
8 eggs
4 T. butter
2 C. Hollandaise sauce

Cook, drain and crumble bacon. Poach eggs. While poaching, slice tomatoes crossways in half. Sauté the half slices of tomatoes in butter, lightly (2 minutes) to a side. Arrange 2 halves on each plate. Cover with crumbled bacon. Place one poached egg on each half tomato. Top with the Hollandaise sauce, and add pepper to taste. ENJOY!

Wink and Sandy Martindale

Cheese Souffle

8 oz. sharp cheddar cheese—
    grated
5 slices white bread
3 eggs—slightly beaten
2 C. milk
1 t. salt
1 t. dry mustard
¼ t. black pepper (optional)

Butter bread generously, remove crusts, and cut into cubes. Layer bread alternately with cheese in buttered casserole dish. Combine eggs, milk, salt, mustard, and pepper and pour over cheese and bread. Let casserole stand overnight in refrigerator. Place in pan of hot water and bake at 350° for 1 hour. Serve immediately. Excellent.

Annie Lee Lasley

Egg Casserole

8 slices bread
1½ lbs. sausage
4 oz. shredded cheddar or Colby
  cheese
4 eggs
2¾ C. milk
1 can Cream of Mushroom soup

Remove crusts and cube bread. Brown sausage. Place bread in bottom of 9 x 13 greased pan and add sausage and cheese. Beat eggs, add milk and soup. Mix well. Pour over bread, sausage, and cheese. Cover with foil and refrigerate overnight. Bake at 350° for 1–1¼ hours. Serves 8.

Margaret Hewitt

Egg Cup with Bacon

6 eggs
6 bacon slices

In a muffin tin, place a strip of bacon around each ring and break an egg into the nest of bacon. Put in hot 450° oven until bacon browns and egg poaches. Serve while hot. This is wonderful for breakfast over the holidays.

Marjorie Lasley Scott

Fish Chowder

1 package haddock filets—
  unthawed
3 C. boiling water
2 C. potatoes—chopped
1 t. salt
¼ t. pepper
4 slices bacon
1 large onion
2 C. milk

Cook fish in water for 10 minutes. Add potatoes, salt, and pepper. Boil 15–20 minutes. Flake fish with a fork. Cook bacon, remove, cook onions in bacon grease. Add to fish. Add milk, crumble bacon into chowder. Heat. Do not boil.

Jackson Mayor Bob Conger

Meats

Sausage Mushroom Casserole

2½ C. seasoned croutons
1½ lbs. bulk sausage
2¼ C. milk
4 eggs
1 can cream of mushroom soup
1 6 oz. can sliced mushrooms
¾ t. dry mustard
2 C. shredded cheddar cheese

Sprinkle croutons in lightly greased 13 x 9 inch baking dish; set aside. Brown sausage, drain and sprinkle over croutons. In large bowl mix milk, eggs, cream of mushroom soup and dry mustard. Pour mixture over sausage. Arrange sliced mushrooms on top of mixture to look pretty. Refrigerate at least 8 hours or overnight. Bake in 325° oven for 50 to 55 minutes. Spread cheddar cheese over top and bake 5 more minutes.

Juanita Shaw

Lasagne

1-1½ lbs. ground beef
1 32 oz. jar spaghetti sauce
8 oz. lasagne noodles
2 eggs
3 C. small curd cottage cheese
½ C. Parmesan cheese
2 T. parsley flakes
½ t. salt and pepper
1 lb. Mozzarella cheese (sliced thin)

Brown ground beef and drain. Add spaghetti sauce. Warm these two together.

For filling, mix together the eggs, cottage cheese, Parmesan cheese, parsley flakes, salt and pepper.

Spray a 9 x 13 inch pan with Pam. Layer ½ noodles, ½ filling, ½ Mozzarella cheese, ½ meat sauce. Repeat layers. Sprinkle additional Parmesan cheese on top. Bake, covered, in a 375° oven for 45 minutes to 1 hour.

Rosie Hayes

Chicken and Broccoli Casserole

1 bunch fresh broccoli
4 large chicken breasts
1 can cream of chicken soup
½ C. mayonnaise
2 T. lemon juice
½ t. curry powder
6 oz. Velveeta cheese, grated

Boil or bake chicken breasts, remove from bone and cut in serving size pieces. Cook broccoli until tender crisp. Layer broccoli and chicken in a 9 x 13 inch pyrex baking dish. Mix soup, mayonnaise, lemon juice and curry powder and spread over chicken and broccoli. Top with grated cheese and bake uncovered in a 350° oven until hot and bubbly (approximately 30 to 40 minutes). Serve with cooked rice. Serves 6-8.

Margaret Hewitt

Hearty Hamburger Chowder

1 C. chopped onions
2 T. butter or shortening
1 lb. ground beef
1 t. salt
⅛ t. pepper
2 C. tomato juice (I like to use V-8)
½ C. chopped green peppers
1 C. sliced carrots
1 C. diced potatoes
1 quart milk
⅓ C. flour

Cook veggies, onions, carrots and pepper in shortening until tender but not brown. Add beef. Cook until crumbly. Stir in juice, potatoes and seasoning. Cover and simmer until vegetables are tender. Combine flour with 1 C. of the milk. Stir into soup mixture. Add rest of the milk and continue cooking on low heat for 20-25 minutes. Serves 6.

Dot Jerstad

Taco Soup

1½ lbs. ground beef
1 large onion, chopped
1 (28 oz.) can whole tomatoes with juice, chopped
1 (14 oz.) can kidney beans, undrained
1 (17 oz.) can whole corn, undrained
1 (8 oz.) can tomato sauce
1 pkg. taco seasoning mix
Salt and pepper
4 cup water

Brown beef and onion in skillet; drain. Combine with other ingredients on large soup pot. Simmer 1 hour.

Serving suggestion: Top with grated cheese and/or sour cream and with corn chips. Serves 8-10.

Sara Elaine Laman

Desserts

Tennessee Jam Cake
(over 100 years old)

5 eggs—separated
1 C. sugar
1 T. soda
1 T. cinnamon
1 T. Allspice
3 C. all-purpose flour
1 C. butter
1 C. blackberry jam
1 C. strawberry jam
1 C. fig preserves
1 C. buttermilk
1 C. pecans—chopped

Cream butter and sugar, add jam and preserves. Add well-beaten egg yolks and beat until smooth. Sift together flour, soda, cinnamon, and Allspice. Add flour mixture and milk alternately and mix well after each addition. Add nuts, fold in egg whites which have been beaten stiff. Bake in three layers.

Filling:

1 C. buttermilk
2 C. sugar
½ t. soda
½ C. butter
½ C. brown sugar
1 T. vanilla

Mix sugar, soda, milk, and butter. Cook until soft ball forms in water. Cool, add vanilla and beat until creamy.

Serena Mitchell

Mother's Jam Cake

1½ C. sugar
3 C. cake flour
1 C. buttermilk
1 t. cinnamon
1 t. nutmeg
½ t. salt
4 eggs
¾ C. butter
1 t. spice
1 t. soda
2 cups jam

Cream butter, sugar, and eggs together until fluffy. Sift flour, measure, add other dry ingredients, and sift together. Add alternately to butter and sugar with buttermilk. Add jam. Turn into 3 . . . 8 inch layers and bake.

Put 12 tablespoons batter in pans for 3 layers. Bake at 350–375 degrees for 30 min.

Desserts

Mother's Date Nut Filling for Jam Cake

1 C. brown sugar
¼ C. butter
½ package of dates
1 box powdered sugar
¾ C. water
⅛ t. salt
1½ C. nuts

Combine sugar, butter, water and dates. Cook until thick. Add the powdered sugar and beat until creamy. Add nuts and salt. Ice cake with filling.

Becky Locke

Fresh Apple Date Cake

2 C. sugar
1½ C. oil
3 eggs
3 C. all purpose flour
1 t. soda
1 t. baking powder
1 t. salt
1 t. ground cinnamon
1 t. ground nutmeg
2 t. vanilla
3 C. chopped firm apples
1 C. chopped pitted dated
1 C. chopped pecans

Icing:

½ C. butter
1 8 oz. package cream cheese
1 box confectioners sugar
Vanilla
Sprinkle nuts on top

Glaze:

¼ C. butter
1 3 oz. package cream cheese
Confectioners sugar to make stiff or
    spreadable
Vanilla
Sprinkle nuts on top

Combine sugar and oil in large bowl. Mix well. Add eggs, one at a time, beating well after each addition. Combine dry ingredients and stir into oil mixture. Add vanilla, apples, dates and pecans and mix well. Use 10 inch tube pan. Bake in a 325° oven for 1½ hours.

Elizabeth Harris

Hummingbird Cake

3 C. all-purpose flour
2 C. sugar
1 t. salt
1 t. soda
1 t. cinnamon
3 eggs—well beaten
1½ C. vegetable oil
1½ t. vanilla
8 oz. can crushed pineapple—
    undrained
2 C. chopped pecans
2 C. chopped bananas

Combine dry ingredients in large mixing bowl, add eggs and salad oil. Stir until moistened. Do not beat. Stir in vanilla, pineapple, 1 C. pecans, and bananas. Spoon batter into 3 well-greased and floured 9″ cake pans. Bake 25 to 30 minutes at 350°. Cool in pans 10 minutes.

Frosting:

2 8 oz. packages cream cheese—
    softened
1 C. softened butter or margarine
2 16 oz. packages powdered sugar
2 t. vanilla

Frost cake and sprinkle with 1 C. chopped pecans.

Margaret Hewitt

Fresh Apple Cake

2 C. sugar
1½ C. Wesson oil
2 eggs
1 t. salt
1 t. soda
½ t. baking powder
1 t. vanilla
3 C. chopped fresh apples (peeled)
½ C. chopped cherries (not
    candied)
1 C. crushed pineapple (drained)
1 C. chopped pecans
3 C. all purpose flour

Cream sugar and oil. Add beaten eggs and mix well. Add salt, soda, baking powder, and vanilla. Beat well. Then add fresh apples, cherries, pineapple, and nuts. Mix well. Then add flour a little at a time, blending well after each addition. Bake in tube pan at 350° for 1½ hours.

Kelley Walker

Sheath Cake

2 C. cake flour
2 C. sugar
½ C. Crisco
1 stick margarine
1 C. water
4 T. cocoa
1 t. vanilla
1 t. soda
½ C. buttermilk
2 eggs—slightly beaten

Place flour and sugar in large bowl. In a pan, mix Crisco, margarine, water and cocoa. Bring to rapid boil and pour over the sugar and flour mixture. Mix well and add vanilla, soda, buttermilk, and eggs. Mix well. Bake in a 2 x 9 x 13 inch pan which has been greased and floured. Bake at 350° for 30 to 40 minutes.

Icing:

4 T. cocoa
6 T. milk
1 stick margarine
1 t. vanilla
1 box confectioners sugar
1 C. pecans—broken

Put cocoa, milk, and margarine in a pan and bring to a boil. Remove from heat and add confectioners sugar, nuts and vanilla. Spread on cake while cake is hot and still in pan. When cool, cut into squares.

Katharine Goodson

Sheath Cake

2 C. flour
2 C. sugar
1 stick margarine
3 T. cocoa
1 C. water
½ C. Crisco
2 eggs
½ C. buttermilk
1 t. soda
1 t. vanilla

Mix flour and sugar together in large bowl. Heat and boil the other ingredients. Mix this with the dry ingredients. Add eggs, buttermilk, soda, and vanilla. Bake 20 minutes in loaf pan at 400°.

Icing:

1 stick margarine
3 T. cocoa
6 T. milk
1 box confectioners sugar
1 t. vanilla

Mix cocoa into melted margarine. Add remaining ingredients. Mix well and pour over hot cake.

Geni Holmes

Chocolate Sheath Cake

2 C. sugar
2 C. flour
1 C. water
1 stick oleo
2 heaping t. cocoa
½ C. oil
2 eggs
½ C. buttermilk
1 t. soda
1 t. vanilla

Mix sugar thoroughly. Bring water, oleo, cocoa, and oil to a boil. Pour over sugar and flour and stir. Add eggs, buttermilk, soda, and vanilla. Pour into greased 9 x 13 pan and bake ½ hour. Frost while hot.

Frosting:

1 stick oleo—melted
2 T. cocoa
⅓ C. milk
1 box powdered sugar
1 t. vanilla

Stir cocoa into melted oleo. Add milk and bring to a boil. Add sugar and vanilla. Beat until smooth and pour over cake as soon as taken out of oven.

Margaret Hewitt

Mother's Devil's Food Cake

4 eggs
⅔ C. butter
2 C. sugar
2 C. flour
1 t. baking powder
1 C. sour milk
1 t. soda (dissolved in milk)
4 T. cocoa
4 T. hot water

Mix sugar, cocoa, cream with butter, then add one egg at a time. Sift dry ingredients, and add alternately with milk. Add hot water last if needed. Makes 3 large round layers. Bake at 350° for 30–35 minutes.

Becky Locke

Icing for Devil's Food Cake

1 lb powdered sugar
4 T. cocoa
1 t. vanilla
½ C. strong coffee

Mix sugar, cocoa, and vanilla with fork. Add just enough strong coffee to thin icing so it will be soft enough to spread on cake.

Becky Locke

Desserts

Chocolate Chip Cake

1 box yellow cake mix
1 small box chocolate instant
   pudding
1 small container or 1 C. sour cream
3 eggs
¾ C. oil
¾ C. water

Blend ingredients for 2 minutes. Add a 6 oz. package of mini-chocolate chips and ½ C. chopped pecans. Bake in a 350° oven for 1 hour in a bundt pan or a tube pan that has been sprayed with Pam.

Gloria Roberts

Orange Slice Cake

2 C. chopped pecans
1 lb. orange slices
1 8 oz. package dates
1 can coconut
1 C. butter (not oleo)

Melt butter and pour over other ingredients. Mix the following ingredients and pour over first mixture.

4 eggs
1½ C. sugar
½ C. buttermilk
1 t. soda
2 C. plain flour

Mix well. Use a greased and floured tube pan. Bake 1½ to 2 hours at 300° or bake until firm. Cake stays fresh for several days and freezes well.

Maxine Crumby

-93-

Heavenly Hash Fudge Cake

1 stick butter
1 square unsweetened chocolate
2 eggs—beaten
1 t. baking powder
1 C. sugar
1 C. flour
½ t. vanilla
1 C. nuts

Melt butter and chocolate together. Add sugar to eggs. Pour into chocolate mixture. Add flour which has been mixed with baking powder, vanilla, nuts. Pour into greased and floured oblong cake pan. Bake at 325° for 30 minutes. Frost while warm.

Frosting:

1 package marshmallows
1 stick butter
1 square unsweetened chocolate
¼ C. warm milk
1 box confectioners sugar

Place marshmallows on top of hot cake. Melt butter and chocolate in milk. Blend in sugar. Pour over marshmallows and swirl together.

Sharon Deaton

Chocolate Marvel

1½ C. flour
3 T. sugar
1 stick margarine
1 C. chopped pecans
1 carton Cool Whip
1 8 oz. package cream cheese
1 package powdered sugar
1 package Vanilla instant pudding
   mix
1 package Chocolate instant
   pudding mix
2¾ C. milk
1 candy bar (milk chocolate)

Mix together flour, sugar, margarine, and pecans. Pat into 9 x 12 inch pan. Bake at 350° until brown, let cool. Combine about 4 oz. Cool Whip, cream cheese, and powdered sugar. Spread over crust. Combine instant puddings and milk. Spread on top of first mixture. Spread remaining Cool Whip over mixture. Shave chocolate bar over top and refrigerate at least 4 hours.

Donna Schrivner

Desserts

Chocolate Delight Cake

1½ C. plain flour
1¼ C. sugar
1 t. salt
1 t. soda
½ t. baking powder
½ C. Crisco
2 squares unsweetened chocolate
1½ C. milk—halved
2 eggs
1 t. vanilla

Combine dry ingredients. Add Crisco, melted chocolate and ¾ C. milk. Mix well. Add eggs, remaining ¾ C. milk and vanilla. Beat on high speed. Pour into pans and bake 30 minutes at 350°. Frost with chocolate icing.

Geni Holmes

Chocolate Pudding Cake

2 T. cocoa
¾ C. sugar
1 C. flour
2 t. baking powder
2 T. oleo
1 t. vanilla
½ C. milk

Mix together and pour into buttered pan (8 x 9 inch).

1 C. brown sugar
2 T. cocoa
1 C. hot water

Mix and sprinkle over batter. Pour hot water over mixture. DO NOT STIR. Bake at 350° for 30 minutes.

Chips Ahoy Cake

1 package yellow cake mix
1 small vanilla instant pudding
4 eggs—beaten
½ C. oil
½ C. water
1 small carton sour cream
1 bar German Sweet Chocolate—
    grated
6 oz. chocolate chips
3 oz. butterscotch chips
1 C. nuts—chopped

Mix all ingredients together. Bake in a greased and floured bundt pan for 55 minutes.

Donna Schrivner

Chocolate Roll

4 egg whites
⅔ C. sugar
4 egg yolks
1 t. vanilla
⅓ C. all-purpose flour
¼ C. cocoa
¼ t. salt
½ t. baking powder

Beat egg whites stiff but not dry; whip in the sugar gradually. Beat egg yolks lightly, add vanilla and beat into the sugar mixture. Fold into this mixture the sifted dry ingredients. Turn into a very shallow pan, 10" x 13", which has first been greased, then lined with waxed paper which has also been greased. Bake at 375° for 15 minutes. Turn out on a cloth rubbed with confectioner's sugar.

Immediately peel off the paper, trim off edges of cake, sift confectioners sugar over the top, and quickly roll up in the cloth like a jelly roll. Then as quickly, unroll to remove cloth; then roll again. Cover with the cloth and set aside until ready to fill, which may be several hours. When ready, unroll and spread with slightly sweetened whipped cream and roll again. Set in refrigerator for filling to get firm. Slice and serve with chocolate sauce.

Eleanor Lasley Haskins

Good Chocolate Dessert

1 C. flour
1 stick margarine
1 C. pecans

Melt margarine and mix with flour and pecans. Press in 9 x 13 inch pan. Bake at 350° until light brown. Cool.

1 8 oz. package cream cheese
1 C. powdered sugar
1 large Cool Whip

Mix ingredients and spread onto cooled crust.

1 large vanilla instant pudding
1 large chocolate instant pudding
3 C. cold milk

Mix together and spread over cream cheese mixture.

1 small Cool Whip
1 T. sugar
1 Hershey bar—grated

Mix Cool Whip with sugar and spread over top. Sprinkle Hershey bar over top of all. Chill and serve.

Gwen Mallard

Carrot Cake

2 C. sugar
4 eggs
2 C. plain flour
2 t. cinnamon
2 t. baking powder
2 t. soda
1 t. salt
1½ C. Wesson Oil
3 C. carrots—finely grated
1 C. pecans—chopped
1 t. vanilla

Cream together sugar, eggs, flour, cinnamon, baking powder, soda, salt, and oil. Add carrots, pecans, and vanilla. Cook in layer pans at 350° until golden brown. Test for doneness with toothpick in center of each layer.

Icing:

8 oz. package Philadelphia cream
  cheese
1 box confectioner's sugar
½ stick butter
2 t. vanilla

Mix and spread on cooled layers.

Connie Haskins

Angel Food Delight

5 egg yolks
1 C. orange juice
½ C. sugar
3 T. lemon juice
1 package Knox gelatin
½ C. boiling water
5 egg whites
¾ C. sugar
2 orange rinds—grated
1 Angel Food cake—pulled into
  pieces
1 carton Cool Whip

Combine egg yolks, orange juice, ½ C. sugar, and lemon juice and cook until thick. Dissolve gelatin in water. Add to pudding. Cool. Beat egg whites and ¾ C. sugar (adding gradually) and orange rind. Arrange layers of Angel Food cake alternately with filling in tube pan. Freeze. Remove from pan and ice with Cool Whip.

Joyce Jones

Cheese Cake

3 eggs—well beaten
2 8 oz. packages cream cheese—
   soft
1 C. sugar
¼ t. salt
2 t. vanilla
½ t. almond flavoring
2⅔ C. sour cream

Combine eggs, cheese, sugar, salt, and flavoring, beat until smooth. Blend in cream. Pour in crumb crust. Bake 35 minutes at 350°. Cool in pan 4 or 5 hours. Chill well.

Crumb Crust:

1¾ C. Graham cracker crumbs
¼ C. walnuts—chopped
½ t. cinnamon
½ C. melted butter

Mix together and press into tube pan. Save 3 T. crumbs for topping.

Joyce Jones

Cream Cheese Cake

1 lb. cream cheese
3 eggs
⅔ C. sugar
2 t. vanilla
1 C. sour cream
3 T. sugar

Beat softened cream cheese, eggs, sugar, and 1 t. vanilla until smooth. Pour into 9 inch pie plate. Bake in 350° oven for 25 minutes. Cool 25 minutes. Mix sour cream, 3 T. sugar and 1 t. vanilla and pour over the top of cheese cake and return to 350° oven for 10 minutes. Cool and chill.

Becky Locke

Strawberry Angel Cake

1 angel food cake
1 can strawberry pie filling
1 8 oz. package cream cheese
½ C. milk
8 oz. whipped topping

Cube angel food cake. Layer ½ in 9 x 13 inch pan. Put strawberry pie filling on top. Add remaining cake.
Mix together cream cheese and milk. Fold in whipped topping.
Freeze. Take out an hour before serving.

Sandra Magee

Coca Cola Cake

2 C. self-rising flour
2 C. sugar
2 sticks butter
3 T. cocoa
1 C. Coca Cola
½ C. buttermilk
2 eggs—beaten
1 t. vanilla
1½ C. miniature marshmallows

Combine flour and sugar. Heat butter, cocoa, and Coca Cola until boiling. Pour over sugar and flour mixture, mixing well. Add milk, eggs, vanilla, and marshmallows. Beat well. Pour into greased and floured pan. Bake 30 to 40 minutes at 350°. Ice cake while hot.

Icing:

1 C. chopped pecans
3 T. cocoa
1 box powdered sugar
½ C. butter
6 T. Coca Cola

Combine butter, cocoa, and Coca Cola. Bring to a boil. Pour over sugar and beat well. Add nuts. Spread on hot cake.

Georgie Mallard

Coconut Cake

1 box Duncan Hines yellow cake
 mix
¼ C. Wesson Oil
3 eggs—beaten
8 oz. sour cream
¾ C. water

Mix all the above well in a large bowl. Grease and flour three 8 inch cake pans. Bake as directed. Cool 5 minutes.

Frosting:

2 C. sugar
½ C. water
1 bag frozen coconut—thawed
4 egg whites—room temperature
¼ t. cream of tartar
2 C. sugar
1 t. vanilla

Cook first 2 ingredients on medium heat until a soft ball is formed when dropped from teaspoon into cold water. Beat egg whites and cream of tartar until soft peaks form. Pour hot syrup over egg whites beating constantly until peaks form. Fold in powdered sugar and vanilla. Spread frosting between cake layers, sprinkle thawed coconut between each layer. Frost side and top with remaining coconut. (This cake tastes like a fresh coconut cake and is very easy to make.)

Celia Willard Collins

Coconut Pound Cake

2 C. sugar
1 C. Crisco oil
5 eggs
2 C. cake flour
½ t. salt
1½ t. baking powder
½ C. sweet milk
1 t. coconut flavoring
1 t. almond flavoring
1 t. vanilla flavoring
1 can Angel Flake coconut

Cream sugar, oil, salt, and baking powder. Add eggs one at a time and beat well. Alternate with flour and milk. Add flavoring and coconut. Bake in greased and floured tube pan for 1 hour at 350°.

Glaze:

1 C. sugar
½ C. butter
½ C. water
1 t. coconut flavoring

Mix glaze ingredients and bring to a boil. When cake is done, pour boiling glaze over cake very slowly. Allow cake to cool completely before removing from pan.

Norma Wilson

White Chocolate Cake

4 oz. white chocolate
½ C. boiling water
1 C. butter or margarine
2 C. sugar
4 egg yolks—unbeaten
1 t. vanilla
2½ C. sifted cake flour
½ t. salt
1 t. soda
1 C. buttermilk
4 egg whites—stiffly beaten

Melt chocolate in boiling water. Cool. Cream butter and sugar until fluffy. Add egg yolks, one at a time, and beat well after each. Add melted chocolate and vanilla. Mix well. Sift together flour, salt, and soda. Add alternately with buttermilk to chocolate mixture; beat well until smooth. Fold in egg whites. Pour in 3 deep 8 or 9 inch pans, lined with waxed paper. Bake in moderate oven (350°) 30–40 minutes. Cool. Frost tops only.

Janette T. Lasley

Rich White Chocolate Frosting

4 oz. white chocolate
2 T. butter
Dash of salt
2 C. confectioner's sugar
2 T. hot water
1 egg yolk
½ t. vanilla

Melt chocolate, blend in sugar, salt and hot water. Add yolk; beat well. Add butter 1 T. at a time; beating thoroughly after each. Stir in vanilla. Makes about ¾ C. or enough to frost tops of two layers.

Janette T. Lasley

White Chocolate Cake

¼ lb. white chocolate
1 C. oleo
2 C. sugar
4 egg yolks
1 t. vanilla
2 C. cake flour
1 t. baking powder
1 C. buttermilk
4 egg whites—beaten til peaks
½ C. chopped pecans
1 C. coconut

Melt chocolate over hot water and cool slightly. Cream butter and sugar. Add melted chocolate. Add egg yolks and beat well. Stir together flour and baking powder. Add flour mixture alternately with buttermilk, beating well. Fold in beaten egg whites, vanilla, pecans, and coconut. Bake at 350° about 30 minutes. Makes a three layer cake.

Icing:

2 C. sugar
2 sticks oleo
1 small can evaporated milk
1 t. vanilla

Cook 20 minutes til soft ball stage. Cool slightly, then beat till thick enough to spread on cake.

JoAnne Alford

Sour Cream Pound Cake

3 C. sugar
3 C. cake flour
2 sticks oleo
6 eggs—separated
1 8 oz. sour cream
½ t. salt
¼ t. soda
1 t. vanilla

Sift flour, soda and salt. Cream butter and sugar. Add vanilla and one yolk at a time. Alternating flour and sour cream. Beat egg whites stiff; fold in. Bake 1 hour and 15 minutes at 350° in greased tube pan.

Anne L. Shaw

Buttermilk Pound Cake

3 C. sifted flour
¼ t. soda
1 C. butter or margarine
2¾ C. sugar
4 eggs
1 C. buttermilk
1 T. grated lemon rind or
1 t. vanilla flavoring or both

Cream butter or margarine and sugar until well blended. Add eggs one at a time, beating well after each until light and fluffy. Mix in lemon rind or add vanilla to buttermilk. Sift flour and soda together and add alternately with milk. Pour into greased tube pan and bake at 350° for 1 hour 10 minutes.

Margaret Hewitt

Old Fashioned Gingerbread

2¼ C. all purpose flour
¾ C. sugar
1 t. soda
½ t. baking powder
2 t. ginger
1 t. cinnamon
¼ t. cloves
½ t. salt
¾ C. soft butter
¾ C. water
2 T. molasses

Pour batter into a greased 9 x 9 x 12 inch baking pan. Bake at 350° for 30–40 minutes or until gingerbread springs back when lightly touched in center. Serve warm.

Judy Martin

Old Fashioned Cake

1 C. butter or oleo
2 C. sugar
6 eggs
1 C. orange juice
4 C. chopped nuts
4 C. flour
½ t. nutmeg

Cream butter and sugar, add egg yolks. Sift dry ingredients together, leaving ½ C. flour for flouring nuts. Add dry ingredients alternating with orange juice. Add nuts. Fold in stiffly beaten egg whites, pour into well-greased tube cake pan and bake in slow oven for 3 hours at 235°. Dust with powdered sugar while still warm. Needs no icing.

Dolly Mathis

Sweet Potato Cake

1½ C. Wesson Oil
2 C. sugar
4 eggs—separated
4 T. hot water
1½ C. grated sweet potatoes
1 C. chopped nuts
1 t. vanilla
2½ C. sifted cake flour
¼ t. salt
3 t. baking powder
1 t. nutmeg
1 t. cinnamon

Combine sugar and oil, blend until smooth. Add egg yolks then hot water. Add dry ingredients that have been sifted together. Add potatoes, vanilla and nuts and beat well. Beat egg whites until stiff. Fold into mixture. Bake in 3 greased 8 inch cake pans at 350° for 25–30 minutes.

Frosting:

1 C. sugar
1 can milk—large
1 stick butter
3 egg yolks
1 can Angel Flake coconut
1 t. vanilla

Cook sugar, milk, butter, and egg yolks on medium heat until mixture thickens (about 12 minutes). Add coconut and vanilla and beat until cool, then frost cake.

Shirley Pounds

Apple Dapple Cake

1½ C. Wesson Oil
2 C. sugar
3 eggs
2 t. vanilla
3 C. flour
1 t. salt
1 t. soda
1½ C. nuts
3 C. raw apple—grated fine

Mix oil, sugar, eggs, and vanilla. Add flour, salt, and soda. Fold in nuts and apple. Bake in tube pan greased well, at 350° for 1½ hours.

Topping:

1 C. packed brown sugar
¼ C. milk
1 stick oleo

Mix and cook 3 minutes. Pour over hot cake. Leave in pan until completely cool.

Serena Mitchell

Carrot Nut Cake

2 C. sifted flour
2 t. baking powder
1 t. baking soda
1 t. salt
2 t. cinnamon
1 C. corn oil
2 C. sugar
4 eggs
3 C. grated raw carrots
1 C. chopped nuts

Sift together flour, baking powder, baking soda, salt, and cinnamon. Add sugar to oil gradually beating well after each addition. Beat eggs until very light. Beat a little at a time into sugar and oil mixture and beat until smooth and fluffy. Gradually stir in sifted dry ingredients, add carrots and nuts, mix well. Pour into two 9" greased and floured pans or tube pan. Bake at 325° for 60 to 65 minutes.

Margaret Hewitt

Happy Day Cake

2½ C. flour—sifted
3 t. Calumet Baking Powder
1 t. salt
1½ C. sugar
½ C. Crisco shortening—room
    temperature
1 C. milk
1 t. vanilla
2 large eggs

Sift flour, baking powder, salt and sugar. Stir shortening just to soften. Add dry ingredients, ¾ C. of milk and vanilla. Mix until all flour is dampened. Beat 2 minutes at medium speed with electric mixer or 300 vigorous strokes by hand. Add eggs and remaining ¼ C. of milk. Beat 1 minute longer with mixer or 150 strokes by hand. Pour batter into two 9 inch layer pans which have been lined on bottom with waxed paper. Bake at 350° for 25 to 30 minutes or until cake tester inserted in center comes out clean. Cool, then frost if desired.

Ethelyn Barlow

Banana Split Cake

1st layer:

2 C. graham cracker crumbs or
   vanilla wafers
1 stick margarine
½ C. powdered sugar

Mix cookie crumbs and melted margarine, or graham cracker crumbs, margarine, and sugar. Press into 9 x 12 x 2 inch pan for crust.

2nd layer:

2 C. powdered sugar
2 egg whites
1 stick margarine

Beat sugar, egg whites, and margarine together for 10 minutes and pour over first layer.

3rd layer:

4–5 bananas
1 lg. can crushed pineapple—
   drained
1 lg. container Cool Whip
Chopped walnuts
Cherries (optional)

Slice bananas over top of 2nd layer of cake. Spread pineapple over bananas, and Cool Whip over all. Top with nuts and cherries. Refrigerate.

Waldorf Cake

½ C. butter
2 C. sugar
1½ C. milk
4 squares Bakers chocolate
2 eggs
2 C. flour
2 t. baking powder
1½ t. vanilla
1 C. nuts

Mix cake ingredients well. Pour into greased pans for 2 thick layers or 3 thin layers. Bake at 350° for 30–35 minutes.

Connie Haskins

Icing:

1 box confectioner's sugar
3 T. cocoa
¼ lb. butter
2 T. cold coffee
1 egg white—beaten
1 t. vanilla

Desserts

One Minute Chocolate Icing

2 T. cocoa
1 C. sugar
¼ C. sweet milk
1 stick oleo
1 t. vanilla flavoring

Melt oleo, add sugar, cocoa, and milk, and mix well. Let come to a rolling boil and boil one minute, no longer; stirring constantly. Add vanilla flavoring. Beat until thick enough to spread. Will ice one two-layer cake. For thicker icing, use 1½ recipes.

Eleanor Haskins

Boiled Frosting

2 C. granulated sugar
2 C. water
3 egg whites
1 t. vanilla, lemon, or almond
  extract

Stir sugar and water until dissolved. Boil until thread stage or 246° F. with thermometer. Slowly pour mixture, while hot, into stiffly beaten egg whites, beating constantly. Add flavoring.

Lillie Mason

Seven Minute Icing

1½ C. sugar
2 egg whites
1½ t. light corn syrup
⅓ C. cold water
Pinch of salt

Beat all ingredients for one minute in the top of a double boiler. Place over boiling water and cook, beating constantly for about 7 minutes or until mixture will form and hold stiff peaks. Remove from heat and add 1 t. pure vanilla. Beat until you have spreading consistency. Frost the tops and sides of one jam cake.

Beverly Shaw Buntin

Desserts

Lemon Cake Pudding

¾ C. granulated sugar
4 T. flour
Pinch of salt
2 eggs—separated
2 t. grated lemon rind
2 T. lemon juice
1 T. melted butter
¾ C. milk

Mix together dry ingredients, flour, sugar and salt. Beat egg yolks until light. Add lemon rind, lemon juice, melted butter and milk. Beat well. Combine with dry ingredients. Beat until smooth. Beat egg whites until stiff, then fold into batter carefully. Pour into well-buttered casserole dish. Place casserole in pan of warm water and bake in preheated 375° oven for 40–50 minutes. As the cake pudding bakes, it separates into a lemon pudding topped with fluffy cake-like layer top. Chill and serve in sherbet glasses or in small plates with or without whipped cream.

Mildred Harris

Orange Cake

1 C. butter
2 C. sugar
4 eggs—room temperature
3½ C. plain flour
½ t. salt
1 t. soda
1¼ C. buttermilk
1 t. vanilla
Grated rind of 1 orange
8 oz. dates
1 C. chopped nuts

Cream shortening until light and fluffy. Add sugar slowly. Add eggs one at a time, beating well after each. Combine flour, salt, and baking soda, mix well. Add flour and buttermilk alternately to mixture. Add orange rind, chopped nuts, dates, and vanilla. Pour into a well-greased 9 or 10 inch tube pan. Bake at 325° for 1½ hours. When done and turned out of cake pan, punch holes with fork in top of cake and pour glaze over it.

Glaze:

1 C. orange juice
2 C. sugar
2 T. orange rind

Trudy Shaw

Granny Taylor's Pound Cake

2½ sticks oleo (softened)
3 C. sugar
3 C. flour (plain)
1 8 oz. container sour cream
¼ t. soda
6 eggs
Pinch of salt
1 t. vanilla
¼ t. almond flavoring

Mix ingredients together. Cook in a 350° oven for 1 hour. Use tube cake pan.

Clara Richardson

Pineapple Sauce

1 small can crushed pineapple
1½ C. sugar
2 eggs
1 stick butter
2 T. flour

Mix all ingredients together and cook until thick. (Very good served over Granny Taylor's Pound Cake.)

Clara Richardson

Jam Cake

1 C. sugar
¾ C. oleo—softened
3 whole eggs
2 C. self-rising flour
½ pint strawberry jam
1 t. soda
½ C. buttermilk
½ t. allspice
½ t. cinnamon
½ t. cloves
½ C. ground raisins—optional
½ C. coconut
½ C. nuts—chopped

Cream oleo, sugar, add eggs—mix well. Add jam, flour and buttermilk with the 1 t. soda dissolved in it. Add flour and milk alternately. Fold in spices and coconut, nuts—bake in 3 pans at 325° until springs back when touched lightly around edges. Cool layers and spread with filling.

Filling:

2 C. sugar
1½ C. oleo
6 egg yolks

Mix sugar with egg yolks, pour into saucepan that has softened oleo. Cook (stirring) until thick. Remove from heat, add 1 cup coconut, 1 cup raisins (if desired) and 1 cup finely chopped nuts. Cool and spread between layers and over top. Best when made several days before serving. Can be made and frozen for weeks.

Thelma Kemp

Orange Crunch Cake

Crunch layer:

1 C. graham cracker crumbs
½ C. firmly packed brown sugar
½ C. chopped walnuts
½ C. margarine—melted

Heat oven to 350°. Grease and flour two 8 or 9 inch pans. In small bowl, combine crunch layer ingredients until crumbly. Press half of crunch mixture into each floured pan.

Cake:

1 package Pillsbury yellow cake mix
½ C. water
½ C. orange juice
⅓ C. oil
3 eggs
2 T. grated orange peel

In large bowl, blend cake ingredients on low speed until moist. Beat 2 minutes on high speed. Pour batter over crunch layer. Bake at 350° for 30 to 35 minutes. Cool 10 minutes. Remove. Cool

Frosting:

1 can vanilla frosting
1 C. frozen whipped topping
3 T. grated orange peel
1 t. grated lemon peel
11 oz. can mandarine oranges—
    drained or 1 orange—sectioned
    and drained
Mint leaves (if desired)

In small bowl beat frosting until fluffy. Add whipped topping and continue beating until light and fluffy. Fold in grated orange peel and lemon peel.

Place 1 layer crunch side up on serving plate, spread ¼ C. of frosting. Top with remaining layer, crunch side up. Spread top and sides with remaining frosting. Arrange orange sections on top. Garnish with mint leaves.

Popcorn Cake

¼ C. butter
¼ C. vegetable oil
½ lb. (4 C.) mini marshmallows
20 caramels
10 C. popped popcorn (lightly
    seasoned)
½ lb. salted nuts (without skins)
½ lb. M & M candies

In sauce pan, combine butter, oil, marshmallows, and caramels. Stir and melt together on low. In large bowl, combine popcorn and nuts. Add melted ingredients and stir until well coated. Mix in M & M's. Press firmly into lightly oiled 10 inch bundt pan. Cool.

Georgie Mallard

Italian Cream Cake

1 stick oleo
½ C. Crisco
5 whole eggs
2 C. flour
2 C. sugar
1 C. buttermilk
1 t. baking soda
1 can Angel Flake coconut
1 C. chopped pecans
1 t. vanilla

Cream butter, Crisco, and sugar. Add egg yolks and beat. Put baking soda in flour and add alternately with buttermilk to above mixture. Add coconut, beaten egg whites, nuts and vanilla. Bake in three layers for about 25 minutes at 350°. Let cool, then frost.

Frosting:

18 oz. package Philadelphia Cream
    Cheese
1 stick oleo
1 box powdered sugar—sifted
1 t. vanilla

Cream all together and spread on cake layers.

Mary Beth Shaw Crockarell

Hummingbird Cake

2 C. sugar
1½ C. cooking oil
3 eggs
2 C. bananas—chopped
8 oz. can crushed pineapple
1½ t. vanilla
3 C. flour
1 t. cinnamon
1 t. baking soda
1 t. salt
1 C. chopped pecans

In a large bowl, combine sugar, oil, eggs, bananas, pineapple and vanilla. Stir. Add dry ingredients and nuts. Beat well by hand. Bake in a greased and floured tube pan at 350° for 1 hour and 15 minutes.

Frosting:

8 oz. Philadelphia Cream Cheese—
    softened
1 T. butter or oleo
1 t. vanilla
1 box confectioners sugar

Beat cheese, butter and vanilla. Add sifted sugar. Beat until spreadable. Spread on cake.

Emily Shaw Weiland

Use Your Imagination Cookies

½ C. wheat germ
1 C. oatmeal
2½ C. unsifted all-purpose flour
1 t. baking soda
1 t. salt
2½ sticks butter
1 C. firmly packed brown sugar
½ C. honey
1 t. vanilla
2 eggs
1 12 oz. package chocolate chips
½ C. coconut
½ C. walnuts
½ C. pecans
½ C. raisins
1 C. butter brickle

Preheat oven to 375°. Combine oats, wheat germ, flour, baking soda and salt in small bowl: set aside. Combine butter with sugar and vanilla in a large bowl: beat until creamy. Beat in eggs. Gradually add flour mixture: blend well. Stir in chocolate chips, raisins, coconut, honey and nuts. Drop by rounded teaspoonsful onto ungreased cookie sheets. Bake at 375° for 8–10 minutes. Amounts vary. Sometimes, depending on ingredients I have on hand, I might add: Carob covered raisins or Macadamia nuts.

**For: Bruce Jenner
1976 Olympics Decathlon Winner**

Linda Thompson

When Linda Thompson began composing lyrics, she had no idea that the first artist to record one of her songs (composed with David Briggs), would be the country-pop giant, Kenny Rogers. He included Linda's "Our Perfect Song" on his RCA LP, "The Heart of the Matter" released in September, 1985.

Linda's background in writing started at age nine when she began composing poetry. She majored in English and Theatre at Memphis State University, where she put herself through college winning beauty contests.

In addition to her burgeoning writing career, acting in film, television, video, and theatre keeps Linda busy. A regular on the syndicated TV show "Hee Haw," Linda spent many seasons portraying the quintessential "Farmer's Daughter." She appeared in Joan River's feature film, "Rabbit Test," and co-starred as Daisy Mae in the Birmingham, Alabama, Summerfest production of "Lil Abner." Linda has also starred on the television series "Fall Guy," "CHiPs," "Vega$," "Starsky and Hutch," "Fantasy Island," and "Riptide."

Linda considers health and fitness an important aspect of her life. Over the past six years she has become proficient in such sports as snow skiing, water skiing, tennis, swimming, bicycling, and aerobics. She also collects authentic hand crafted soft sculptured dolls from the South and has even found time to name them all.

Linda has two sons, Brandon and Brody, and lives in Southern California.

Oatmeal Chocolate Chip Cookies

½ C. butter
½ C. granulated sugar
¼ C. brown sugar
1 egg
1 t. vanilla
⅔ C. all purpose flour
½ t. salt
1 t. cinnamon
½ t. baking soda
⅛ t. nutmeg
1½ C. quick cooking oats
1 6 oz. package chocolate chips

Cream until soft. Add sugars, egg and vanilla. Beat until light. Blend in flour, soda, salt, and spices. Stir in oats and chips. Drop on ungreased cookie sheets about 2 inches apart. Bake at 375° for 8 minutes or until light brown.

Leigh Ann Jones

Peanut Butter-Oatmeal Cookies

½ stick butter
1 C. peanut butter
2 C. sugar
½ C. milk
3 C. oatmeal

Melt butter and peanut butter. Add sugar and milk. Cook over low heat for about 3 minutes. Add oatmeal, mix well. Drop onto cookie sheet or wax paper. Let harden. Makes 3 dozen.

Geni Holmes

Oatmeal Cookies

1 C. raisins
1 C. water
¾ C. shortening
1½ C. sugar
2 eggs
1 t. vanilla
½ C. nuts
2½ C. flour
1 t. soda
1 t. salt
1 t. cinnamon
½ t. cloves
2 C. oats

Simmer raisins in water over low heat 20–30 minutes. Drain liquid into measuring cup. Heat oven to 400°. Cream shortening and sugar, add eggs and vanilla. Stir in liquid. Sift dry ingredients and stir into mixture; add oats, nuts, and raisins. Drop by teaspoon onto cookie sheet. Bake 8–10 minutes. Makes 6–7 dozen.

Joyce Jones

Desserts

Soft Molasses Cookies

1 C. shortening
1 C. brown sugar—packed
1 C. molasses
4 C. sifted flour
2 eggs
½ C. buttermilk
3 t. ginger
1 t. cinnamon
½ t. nutmeg
½ t. cloves
2 t. salt
2 t. soda

Combine shortening, spices, salt, brown sugar, molasses and eggs. Beat well, sift flour with soda and add to first mixture. Add buttermilk, mix well. Chill dough over night. Roll on floured board. Cut ½ inch thick. Bake on greased cookie sheet at 400° for 8–10 minutes.

Ruth C. Gann

Gingerbread Men

1 C. shortening
1 C. sugar
½ t. salt
1 egg
1 C. molasses
2 T. vinegar
5 C. sifted flour
1 T. ginger
1 t. ground cloves
1½ t. soda
1 t. cinnamon
2 C. confectioners' sugar
Half & half cream
1 small package red hots

Thoroughly cream shortening, sugar and salt. Stir in egg, molasses and vinegar. Beat well. Sift dry ingredients; stir into molasses mixture. Cut with gingerbread man cutter. Place 1″ apart on greased cookie sheet. Bake at 375° about 6 minutes. Cool and remove to a rack. When completely cool, decorate with red hots and confectioners' icing.

Icing:

Add a little half & half cream to confectioners' sugar to make a paste that will go easily through a pastry tube. Makes 4 dozen 6″ gingerbread men.

Barbara Stafford

Gingersnaps

2 C. flour
½ C. sugar
½ t. soda
1 t. salt
½ t. allspice
1 t. ginger
½ t. cinnamon
⅛ t. cloves
⅔ C. molasses
6 T. shortening

Mix together flour, sugar, soda, salt, allspice, ginger, cinnamon and cloves. Heat molasses to boiling. Remove from heat and add shortening and stir until shortening is melted. Add dry ingredients to molasses. Mix well. Chill. Preheat oven to 350°. Roll out dough very thin on floured surface. Cut out and place on greased cookie sheet. Bake 8 minutes. Makes 5 dozen.

Geni Holmes

Southern Tea Cakes

½ C. shortening
½ C. oleo
1½ C. sugar
4 C. plain flour
½ t. salt
1 t. soda
1 t. baking powder
⅓ C. milk
2 eggs
1 t. vanilla

Cream shortening, oleo, sugar and 1 egg at a time. Mix dry ingredients together. Add milk and vanilla. Dough will be real stiff. Chill 1 hour in refrigerator. Roll out on floured pastry cloth or board about ¼ inch thick. Sprinkle with sugar and dot with raisins, nuts, etc. Bake on greased cookie sheet at 350° for 10 to 12 minutes. Put dough back in refrigerator while each batch is cooking.

Georgie Mallard

Old Fashioned Tea Cakes

1 C. sugar
1 stick margarine
2 eggs
1 t. vanilla
2 C. self-rising flour

Mix all ingredients together. Roll out on floured surface until very thin. Cut cookie dough with knife. Placed on greased cookie sheet. Bake 8 minutes at 350°.

Geni Holmes

Sugar Cookies

¾ C. margarine
1 C. sugar
2 eggs
½ t. vanilla
3 C. plain flour
1 t. baking powder
1 t. salt

Cream margarine and sugar until light and fluffy. Blend in eggs and vanilla. Add combined dry ingredients, mix well. Chill 4 hours or overnight. Roll out dough on floured surface to ⅛ inch thickness. Cut with floured cookie cutters, pressing firmly. Place on ungreased cookie sheet. Bake at 400° for 5–7 minutes. Cool slightly before removing from cookie sheet. Makes 4 dozen.

Sue Harvill

Grandmother's Vanilla Drop Cookies

4 C. flour
2 t. baking powder
1½ t. salt
¾ C. shortening—melted
1½ C. sugar
2 t. vanilla
2 eggs—slightly beaten
2 T. milk

Mix shortening and sugar together. Add eggs. Sift dry ingredients and add to sugar mixture alternately with milk. Add vanilla. Drop by spoon onto cookie sheet and bake at 375° for 10 minutes.

Joyce Jones

Snickerdoodles

1 C. soft shortening
1½ C. sugar
2 eggs
2¾ C. sifted flour
2 T. cream of tartar
1 t. soda
½ t. salt
2 t. cinnamon

Blend together shortening, sugar and eggs. Add cream of tartar, soda and salt to flour and sift. Add to creamed mixture. Roll dough in balls the size of walnuts. Roll in mixture of 2 t. cinnamon and 2 T. sugar. Place balls 2 inches apart on ungreased cookie sheet. Bake 8–10 minutes in preheated 400° oven.

Linda Brackett

Mom's Shortbread

½ lb. butter
½ C. very fine granulated sugar
1 egg yolk
1½ C. sifted flour
Pinch of baking soda

Cream butter and sugar together. Add egg yolk, then combine all ingredients. Add more flour until dough kneads nicely. Roll not too thin (about ¼ inch). If first cookie spreads or looks greasy, add more flour and knead. Bake in a moderate (350°) oven 8–12 minutes until light brown.

Margaret Hewitt

Butter Crescents

1 C. butter (not oleo)
5 T. sugar
1 t. vanilla
2 C. flour (plain)
1 T. water
½ t. salt
1 C. chopped pecans

Cream the butter and sugar. Add other ingredients. Form cookies in crescent shape about the size of your finger. Bake on ungreased cookie sheet at 350° to 375° until slightly browned, approximately 10 minutes. Cool and roll in powdered sugar.

Maxine Crumby

Brownies

2 sticks oleo
6-8 T. cocoa
4 eggs
2 C. sugar
1½ C. plain flour
½ t. baking powder
2 t. vanilla

Melt oleo and cocoa. Add eggs and beat. Add flour, baking powder, sugar, and vanilla. Beat well. Pour into 9 x 13 inch greased and floured pan. Bake in a 350° oven for 15-20 minutes.

Frosting:

⅓ stick oleo
3 T. cocoa
3 T. milk
2 C. confectioners sugar
1 t. vanilla

Melt oleo and cocoa. Add milk, confectioners sugar and vanilla. Beat until smooth. Spread over brownies.

Sandra Magee

Fudge Brownies

1 C. flour—unsifted
¼ t. baking soda
½ t. salt
⅓ C. butter
¾ C. sugar
12 oz. package semi-sweet
   chocolate morsels
2 t. pure vanilla extract
2 eggs
2 C. pecan halves
2 T. water

Do not use mixer. Preheat oven to 325°. In small bowl, combine flour, baking soda and salt, and set aside. In small sauce pan, combine butter, sugar and water. Bring to a boil, remove from heat and add ½ of the chocolate morsels and the vanilla. Stir until the mixture is smooth. Transfer to large bowl. Add eggs and flour, stir just enough to moisten. Add nuts and remaining morsels. Bake at 325° for 30 minutes. Cool over night.

Marjorie Schrivner

Dad's Cookies

1 C. white sugar
1 C. brown sugar
1 C. butter or shortening
2 eggs—beaten
¼ t. salt
1 t. vanilla
2 C. flour
1 t. baking powder
1 t. soda
2 C. oatmeal
1½ C. coconut

Cream butter or shortening and work in sugars. Add beaten eggs and vanilla. Sift flour, salt, baking soda, and baking powder, and work in well. Add oatmeal and coconut. Roll into balls and pat with fork. Cook at 325° for 8–10 minutes.

Margaret Hewitt

Caramel Pecan Bars

1 stick butter—melted
1 box brown sugar
2 eggs—beaten well
2 C. flour
2 t. baking powder
¼ t. salt
1 C. chopped pecans
½ C. Angel Flake coconut

Mix butter and sugar, let cool. Add other ingredients. Mix and pour into greased pan 9 x 9 inches and bake at 275° until lightly golden brown. Do not over bake. Cut into bars.

Serena Mitchell

Chess Squares

1 package yellow cake mix
1 stick melted butter
4 eggs
1 8 oz. Philadelphia Cream Cheese
1 lb. powdered sugar

Mix cake mix, melted butter, and 2 eggs and press into bottom of greased pan. Mix powdered sugar, cream cheese, and 2 eggs on top of first layer. Bake at 375° for 35 minutes. Serves 24.

Leigh Geyer

Lemon Squares

1 C. butter or margarine
2 C. flour
½ C. powdered sugar
¼ t. salt
4 eggs
4 T. flour
2 C. sugar
4 T. lemon juice

Mix first 4 ingredients and bake 20 minutes at 325°. Beat eggs, add other ingredients, and mix well. Pour into baked crust. Bake 25 minutes at 325°. Dust with powdered sugar and cut into squares.

Joyce Jones

Corn Flake Cookies

6 C. corn flakes
1 C. white Karo syrup
1 C. sugar
½ t. vanilla
12 oz. crunchy peanut butter

Put corn flakes in a large bowl. Mix Karo, sugar and vanilla. Bring to a boil. Set aside and add peanut butter.

Pour over corn flakes and mix. Press into a 9 x 11 inch pan. Let set, then cut into squares.

Elizabeth Richardson

Lemon Squares

Step 1:

1½ C. flour
½ C. brown sugar
1 stick margarine

Melt margarine and mix well with other ingredients. Pat out in a square cookie sheet pan. Bake for 10 minutes at 275°.

Step 2:

2 eggs
1 C. brown sugar
1½ C. coconut
1 C. chopped nuts
2 T. self-rising flour
½ t. vanilla

Mix and put on top of first layer. Bake for 20 minutes at 350°.

Step 3: (Icing)

1½ C. confectioners sugar
2 T. melted butter
Juice of 1 lemon

Mix well and spread on top while warm. Thin with milk, if needed. Serves 20–24.

Betty Deere

Lemon-Cheese Bars

1 Duncan Hines Pudding Recipe
   yellow cake mix
1 8 oz. package cream cheese—
   softened
⅓ C. sugar
1 t. lemon juice
⅓ C. Crisco oil
2 eggs

Mix dry cake mix, 1 egg, and ⅓ cup oil until crumbly, reserve 1 cup. Pat remaining mixture lightly in an ungreased 13 x 9 x 2 inch pan. Bake 15 minutes at 350°. Beat cheese, sugar, lemon juice and 1 egg until light and smooth. Spread over baked layer. Sprinkle the reserved crumb mixture. Bake 15 minutes longer. Cool and cut into bars.

Donna Schrivner

Desserts

Melted Moments

1 C. butter or oleo
⅓ C. powdered sugar
¾ C. cornstarch
1 C. plain flour

Icing:

1 3 oz. package cream cheese
1 C. powdered sugar
1 t. vanilla
Food coloring

Mix together, chill until firm. Pinch and roll into 1 inch balls. Place on cookie sheets. Press hole with thumb before they cook. Bake at 350° for 12 minutes. Repress just before done. Frost with icing. Makes 40 cookies.

Leigh Ann Jones Taylor

M & M Cookies

2½ C. plain flour
½ t. soda
½ t. salt
1 C. butter or margarine
¾ C. brown sugar
¾ C. white sugar
1 t. vanilla
2 eggs

Mix together. Crush ½ bag M & M's and add to mixture. Mix well. Top with M & M's just before they are finished baking.

Leigh Ann Jones Taylor

Oatmeal Chocolate Chip Cookies

1 C. Crisco
¾ C. brown sugar
¾ C. granulated sugar

Blend together until light and fluffy.

2 eggs, one at a time, unbeaten
1 t. hot water (a must)

Add eggs and hot water.

1½ C. plain flour
1 t. soda
1 t. salt

Sift together flour, soda and salt.

1 C. chopped pecans
2 C. semi-sweet chocolate chips
2 C. oatmeal (do *not* use quick
    cooking oats)
1 t. vanilla

Blend ingredients well. Drop by half teaspoonfuls on a greased cookie sheet. Bake at 375° for 10 minutes. Do not overbake.

Maxine Crumby

Almond Fingers

1 C. butter—softened
½ C. powdered sugar
1½ C. all-purpose flour—sifted
¼ t. salt
1 t. almond extract
2 C. toasted almonds—chopped

In large bowl of electric mixer, cream together the butter and sugar thoroughly. Add flour sifted with salt, blend well, then beat in flavoring. Stir in almonds; chill about an hour for easier handling. To bake, pinch off about a tablespoon of the mixture and roll between palms of hands into a 2 inch long cylinder about ½ inch thick. Place on lightly greased baking sheet and bake at 325° for 20 minutes, or until very lightly browned. Remove cookies to a flat pan onto which you have sifted powdered sugar, then sift more sugar over top of the cookies. Store in airtight container with waxed paper between layers. Freezes well. Makes about 6 dozen.

Betsy Thompson

Meringue Cookies

2 egg whites—beaten stiff
⅔ C. sugar
1 t. vanilla
Pinch of salt
1½ C. coconut (optional)

Slowly add sugar and salt to egg white beating. Stir in 1½ C. coconut and vanilla. Drop by teaspoonfuls on cookie sheet lined with aluminum foil. Preheat oven to 350°. Put cookies in oven and turn oven off. Leave overnight. Do not open oven door. (Can use 1 C. chocolate chips and 1 C. chopped nuts or other ingredients—chopped dates, etc.)

Margaret Hewitt

Desserts

Kim's Cookies

1 stick butter or margarine
1½ C. graham cracker crumbs
1 C. chocolate chips
1½ C. coconut
1 C. pecans
1 C. sweetened condensed milk

Melt butter in 9 x 13 pan. Layer graham cracker crumbs, chocolate chips, coconut, then pecans. Pour milk over all. Bake at 350° for 25 minutes. Cool and cut in squares.

Kim Brooks

Exotic Bars

1 C. sugar
1 C. butter
½ C. evaporated milk
2 eggs—slightly beaten
2 packages Graham crackers
1 C. coconut
1 C. pecans
1 t. vanilla

Boil sugar, butter, evaporated milk, and eggs until thick. Remove from heat. Add coconut, pecans, and vanilla. Line bottom of 13 x 9 inch pan with Graham crackers. Pour mixture in pan on top of crackers. Top with graham crackers laid flat on top. Place in refrigerator. Mix topping and spread on top of all. Cut into bars.

Leigh Ann Jones

Topping:

2 C. powdered sugar
½ C. butter—melted
2 t. lemon juice

Pecan Crunch Cookies

1 C. butter or margarine
½ C. sugar
1 t. vanilla
½ C. crushed potato chips
½ C. chopped pecans
2 C. sifted all purpose flour

Cream butter, sugar, and vanilla. Add potato chips and pecans. Stir in flour. Form into small balls and flatten with floured tumbler or fork. Place on ungreased cookie sheet and bake at 350° for 16–18 minutes or until lightly browned.

Margaret Hewitt

Oatmeal Cookies

1 C. Old-Fashioned oatmeal
1 C. plain flour
½ C. sugar
1 t. cinnamon
1 stick butter or oleo
1 egg
½ t. soda
2 T. buttermilk
1 t. vanilla
¾ C. pecans—broken
⅔ C. raisins
Marachino cherries—cut in thirds

Mix soda with buttermilk. Blend all ingredients (except cherries) with a spoon by hand in a large bowl. Drop the blended mixture from a small teaspoon onto a greased cookie sheet. Top each cookie with a cherry. Cook at 325° until browned.

Mrs. Swanee Lawrence

Date Balls

1 stick butter
1 egg—well beaten
1 C. sugar
1 sm. package chopped dates
¾ C. pecans
2½ C. Rice Krispies
1 t. vanilla
Coconut

Melt butter, add beaten egg, sugar and dates. Cook in skillet for 6 minutes, stirring constantly. Remove from heat, add Rice Krispies, nuts, and vanilla. Cool and form into balls. Roll in coconut.

Judy Martin

Pecan Pie

2 lg. eggs
½ C. sugar
1 C. dark Karo syrup
4 T. oleo—melted
1 t. vanilla flavoring
2 T. flour
½ C. chopped pecans

Mix together the well-beaten eggs, sugar, syrup, oleo, and flavoring. Stir in flour, mixing well, add pecans. Pour into 9-inch unbaked pie shell. Bake 1 hour at 325°. Cool on rack.

Ethelyn Barlow

Pecan Pie

3 eggs—slightly beaten
1 C. light or dark corn syrup
1 C. sugar
2 T. butter or margarine
1 t. vanilla
1½ C. pecans
1 unbaked 9″ pastry shell

In large bowl, stir together eggs, syrup sugar, butter, and vanilla until well blended. Stir in nuts. Pour into pastry shell. Bake at 350° for 50–55 minutes or until knife inserted halfway between center and edge comes out clean. Cool.

Sarah Lasley Ralls

Pecan Pie

1 C. dark Karo syrup
1 C. sugar
4 whole eggs—well beaten
2 T. flour (heaping)
1 stick oleo
1 C. pecans
1 unbaked pie shell

Mix sugar and flour, add syrup, eggs, and oleo. Pour into pie shell and sprinkle nuts over top. Bake 1 hour at 350°.

Ellen Henderson

Poor Man's Pecan Pie

⅔ C. sugar
⅔ C. white Karo syrup
⅔ C. melted oleo
⅔ C. oatmeal
2 eggs
1 unbaked pie shell

Mix all ingredients and pour in unbaked pie shell. Bake at 350° for 25–30 minutes.

Katharine Goodson

Chess Pie

1½ C. sugar
1½ T. flour
1½ T. meal
1 t. vinegar
¼ C. milk
3 eggs
1 stick butter—melted
1 t. vanilla

Beat eggs. Add sugar, flour, and meal to eggs. Stir. Add vanilla, vinegar and milk. Lastly, add the melted butter. Stir all ingredients well. Put into unbaked pie shell. Bake at 350° for 45-50 minutes until firm in the middle.

Anne L. Shaw

Apple Crisp

4 C. sliced apples
⅔ C. brown sugar
⅔ C. flour
⅓ C. oleo
½ t. cinnamon

Place apples in greased pie plate. Cut oleo into sugar and flour. Mix well and spread over apples. Bake 45 minutes in a 350° oven.

Sandra Magee

Overnight Ice Cream Dessert

¾ C. vanilla wafer crumbs in bottom
    of ungreased 9 x 14 inch pan
2 squares baking chocolate
⅔ C. butter or oleo
2 C. powdered sugar
2 egg yolks
1 t. vanilla
1 C. chopped nuts
2 egg whites, stiffly beaten
½ gallon pecan ice cream
¾ C. vanilla wafer crumbs for
    topping

Melt chocolate with butter or oleo. Add powdered sugar, egg yolks, vanilla and nuts.

Fold in egg whites. Put chocolate mixture on top of crumbs and freeze for two hours. Add ice cream. Spread evenly on top of chocolate. Sprinkle top with remaining vanilla wafer crumbs and freeze.

Maxine Crumby

Torte Pie

6 oz. white sugar
6 oz. brown sugar
¾ C. egg whites
¼ t. cream of tartar
1 t. vanilla
5 oz. graham cracker crumbs
4 oz. pecan pieces
Whipped cream

Combine two sugars. Beat egg whites until stiff, adding sugars gradually while beating. Add vanilla. Fold in crumbs and pecans by hand. Pour in 8 inch round pie pan. Depress middle. Cook at 350° for 25 minutes. Cool. Top with whipped cream.

Maxine Crumby

Chess Pie

½ C. margarine
1½ C. sugar
3 eggs—beaten
1 t. cider vinegar
1 t. vanilla
¼ t. salt
1 8 inch unbaked pastry shell

Melt butter in saucepan. Add sugar and mix until smooth. Stir in eggs, vinegar, vanilla, and salt. Beat to blend ingredients. Pour into pastry shell and bake about 50 minutes at 350°. Makes 6 servings.

Katherine Goodson

Chess Pie

3 eggs
1½ C. sugar
1 stick butter—melted
1 T. meal
1 T. vinegar
1 t. vanilla

Mix and pour into unbaked pie shell. Bake at 350° for 35 minutes. Serves 6.

Leigh Geyer

Chess Pie

1 ½ C. sugar
¼ lb. butter (1 stick)—melted
1½ T. flour
1½ T. meal
3 eggs—beaten
¼ C. cream
1 t. vanilla
½ t. lemon
Pinch of salt

Mix sugar, flour, meal, and salt. Add beaten eggs, cream, flavorings, and melted butter. Bake at 350° for 45–50 minutes.

Elizabeth Harris

Mrs. Ragan's Buttermilk Pie

5 eggs—well beaten
2 C. sugar
¾ C. buttermilk
½ t. vanilla
1 stick butter—melted
1 T. lemon juice
1 unbaked 9″ pie shell

Mix ingredients well. Pour into pie crust and bake at 350° for 30 minutes or until golden brown on top.

Joanne Ragan

Buttermilk Pie

2 C. sugar
1 T. flour
4 eggs
1 stick oleo—melted
⅔ C. buttermilk
1 t. vanilla
Dash of salt

Pour into unbaked 9-inch pie crust. Bake at 325° for 35–40 minutes.

Barbara Jones

Chocolate Chess Pie

2 eggs—well beaten
1½ C. sugar
½ stick oleo
1 sm. can evaporated milk
1 t. vanilla
2 T. cocoa (or less)

Melt oleo and let cool while mixing other ingredients. Combine sugar and chocolate. Stir in milk and eggs and add vanilla and oleo. Stir well. Pour in unbaked pie shell. Bake at 350° for 35 minutes or until firm.

Melinda Wilkins

Old Southern Chocolate Pie

4 eggs—separated
1 C. sweet milk—scalded
1¼ C. sugar
2 T. flour
2 T. butter
Pinch of salt
3 T. cocoa
1 t. pure vanilla

Combine cocoa with the other dry ingredients thoroughly mixed. Mix with all other ingredients and pour into a chilled pie crust. Bake at 400° until custard is firm. (Test with the blade of a knife.) Spread on the meringue made with reserved egg whites. Pile high and swirl with your spoon. Return to the oven to brown.

Beverly Buntin

Chocolate Pie

1½ C. sugar
½ C. flour
2 T. cocoa
4 egg yolks
2 C. milk
1 stick margarine
1 t. vanilla
Pinch of salt

Meringue:

4 egg whites
¼ C. sugar
⅛ t. cream of tartar

Mix sugar, flour, and cocoa together in large saucepan. Add egg yolks and milk. Cook over medium heat until thick, stirring constantly. Add margarine, vanilla, and salt. Pour into 2 baked pie shells.

Beat egg whites, sugar, and cream of tartar until it forms peaks. Spread on top of pies. Bake at 325° until meringue is light brown (about 20 minutes). Makes 2 pies.

Melody Taliaferro

Chocolate Pie

4 egg yolks
3 C. sugar
4 T. cocoa
4 T. flour
2½ C. milk
1 stick oleo
1 t. vanilla

Combine sugar, flour, and cocoa. Add eggs and milk. Cook on top of stove until thick. Add vanilla and oleo. Pour into baked crust and top with meringue. Makes 2 pies.

Peggy Haywood

Chocolate Pie

1½ C. sugar
4 T. cocoa
8 T. flour
1 lg. can evaporated milk
2 C. water
Dash of salt
4 egg yolks—beaten
¼ C. butter
2 unbaked pie shells

Mix sugar, cocoa, flour, and enough milk to mix. Add remaining milk, water, and salt. Stir in egg yolks. Microwave on high until thickened, stirring every 2 minutes. Stir in butter, and pour into pie shells. Top with meringue. Bake at 350° until fairly browned.

Cynthia Grimsley

Chocolate Pie

1 C. milk
¾ C. sugar
2½ T. cocoa
2½ T. flour
½ stick oleo
1 t. vanilla flavoring

Combine ½ of the sugar with the milk and the egg yolks. Bring to a boil in double boiler; then add the rest of the ingredients. Stir until thick.

Agnes Taylor

Barbara Higgs' Chocolate Pie

2 egg yolks—slightly beaten
1 C. sugar
1 C. water
5 T. flour
4 t. cocoa or 3 t. lemon juice
⅓ stick oleo
1 t. vanilla

Mix ingredients well and cook until thick. Add oleo and vanilla; pour into baked pie crust. Top with egg white meringue and brown slightly in oven.

Chocolate Ice Cream Pie

1 package chocolate instant
    pudding
1 package vanilla instant pudding
2 graham cracker crusts
1⅓ C. milk
3 C. vanilla ice cream—softened
Non-dairy whipped topping
Chocolate or Toffee bar—crumbled
    finely

Beat milk and softened ice cream together with electric mixer. Add chocolate pudding mix, beat 2 minutes. Add in vanilla pudding mix, beat 2 minutes. Pour into pie shells; freeze for 2 hours before serving. Top with non-dairy whipped topping and garnish with grated chocolate or toffee bar. Serves 6–8.

Donna Schrivner

Granny's Lemon Pie

1 can Eagle Brand Milk
⅓ cup lemon juice
1 8 oz. Cool Whip
1 chocolate graham cracker
    pie crust

Combine Eagle Brand Milk and lemon juice. Mix with a whisk until well blended. Fold in Cool Whip. Pour into pie crust and chill 1 hour before serving.

Nancy Jane Hall
Jackson, Tennessee

Fudge Pie

2 eggs
1 C. sugar
½ stick butter
1 t. vanilla
⅛ t. salt
½ C. flour
2 squares semi-sweet chocolate

Beat eggs, sugar and flour together. Melt butter and chocolate on low heat. Then add vanilla and salt. Combine two mixtures. Stir; pour into lightly buttered 9-inch pie pan. Bake at 350° for 30 minutes. Serve with whipped cream or ice cream on top. Serves 6.

Deborah Shaw Laman

Banana Fudge Pie

1 15 oz. package pie crust
¾ C. Nestles Little Bit (semi-sweet)
1 8 oz. container La Creme or Cool Whip
2 eggs—beaten
¼ C. sugar
2 medium bananas—sliced

Preheat oven to 350°. In heavy guage saucepan, melt ½ cup Little Bits over low heat. Stir in 1 cup La Creme, eggs, and sugar; mix well. Pour into prepared pie crust. Bake at 350° for 28–32 minutes or until crust is lightly browned. Cool 10 minutes, chill 1 hour. Layer bananas and remaining La Creme over baked layer. Top with remaining Little Bits. Garnish with banana slices if desired. Keep refrigerated.

Sharon Deaton

Sweetheart Fudge Pie

¼ C. butter
¾ C. brown sugar
3 eggs
2 6 oz. packages chocolate chips
2 t. instant coffee
1 t. rum flavoring
¼ C. all purpose flour
1 C. chopped walnuts
1 C. whipping cream
2 T. chopped Maraschino cherries

Cream butter with brown sugar; add eggs, one at a time, beating well. Melt chocolate over hot water. Add to creamed mixture with coffee and rum flavoring. Stir in flour and walnuts. Pour into unbaked pie shell. Bake at 375° for 25 minutes. Cool. Whip cream stiff, add cherries, spread on top of pie. Decorate with chocolate.

Sally Baker

Pumpkin Pie

1 can pumpkin pie filling
1 can Eagle Brand milk
2 eggs
1 t. cinnamon
½ t. salt
½ t. nutmeg
½ t. ginger
1 unbaked pie shell

Mix together and pour in unbaked pie shell. Bake in 425° oven for 15 minutes. Reduce to 350° and bake 25–30 minutes until knife inserted 1″ from edge comes out clean.

Donna Hewitt

Osogood Pie

1 C. sugar
1 C. raisins
½ C. chopped pecans
½ t. cloves
½ t. cinnamon
1 t. vinegar
½ t. salt
2 T. butter
2 eggs—*separated* and beaten
1 unbaked pie shell

Mix all ingredients, folding in whites last. Pour in unbaked pie shell. Bake at 350° 30–35 minutes. Can substitute chopped dates for raisins.

Mr. Ira Johnson

Coconut Angel Pie

16 Graham crackers (1⅓ C.)
½ C. butter—melted
4 egg whites
¼ t. salt
1 t. vanilla
1 C. sugar
1½ C. heavy cream
1 C. shredded coconut
2 T. sugar
1 t. vanilla
1 C. fruit (peaches)

Prepare pie crust by mixing crushed graham crackers and butter, and pressing into pie plate. Beat egg whites, add salt and vanilla and beat until stiff, gradually adding 1 C. sugar (2 T. at a time). Beat thoroughly after each addition. Spread in pie crust. Bake at 375° for 1¼ hours. Cool. Toast ½ C. coconut. Whip cream and fold in remaining coconut. Spread over egg white mixture. Sprinkle with toasted coconut and top with fruit.

Joyce Jones

French Coconut Pie

1 stick butter—melted
3 eggs
1½ C. sugar
1 T. vinegar
1 C. coconut

Mix all ingredients. Pour into unbaked pie shell. Bake for 1 hour at 350°.

Dorothy Mitchell

Never Fail Meringue

2 T. sugar
1 T. cornstarch
½ C. water
3 egg whites
⅛ t. salt
½ t. vanilla
6 T. sugar

Combine 2 T. sugar and cornstarch in saucepan. Add water. Cook over medium heat stirring constantly until mixture is thick and clear. Cool.

Beat 3 egg whites with salt and vanilla until soft mounds form.

Add 6 T. sugar gradually beating well after each addition. Add cornstarch mixture. Continue beating until meringue stands in stiff peaks.

Louise Dent

Buttermilk Coconut Pie

1½ C. sugar (or less)
3 eggs
6 T. buttermilk
½ stick melted butter
1 C. coconut
1 t. vanilla
Pinch of salt

Mix all ingredients together. Place in unbaked pie shell. Bake at 450° for 10 minutes. Reduce heat to 350° and bake 30-35 minutes longer. May need to cover with foil last 10-15 minutes of cooking to prevent top from getting too brown.

Maxine Crumby

Desserts

Jelly Custard Pie

1 unbaked pie crust
2 eggs
1 C. sugar
¼ C. butter
¼ C. plum jelly
½ t. vanilla

Blend all ingredients together, pour into unbaked pie shell. Cook at 350°.

Annie Lee Lasley

Lemon Rub Pie

1 stick butter—softened
1½ C. sugar
1 rounding teaspoon flour
2 lemons
3 eggs—separated

Cream sugar and butter. Add flour, lemon juice and yellow of eggs beaten slightly. Beat egg whites until stiff. Fold into mixture. Put into pie crust that has been cooked 10–12 minutes at 400°. Finish at 350° for 30 minutes.

Pineapple Coconut Pie

4 eggs
1 stick oleo—melted
2 C. sugar
1 t. flour
1 8½ oz. can crushed pineapple—drained
1 C. Angel Flake coconut

Beat eggs. Stir in flour, sugar, and melted oleo. Add drained pineapple and coconut. Pour into unbaked pie shell. Bake at 350° for about 45 minutes or until firm. Makes 2 9-inch pies.

Peanut Butter Crunch Pie

½ C. peanut butter
⅓ C. corn syrup
2 C. Kellogg's Rice Krispies
1 quart vanilla ice cream—slightly soft

Measure peanut butter and corn syrup into mixing bowl. Mix until thoroughly combined. Add Rice Krispies cereal, stir until well coated. With back of tablespoon, press mixture evenly and firmly in bottom and around sides of lightly buttered 9-inch pan to form crust. Chill until firm. Spread ice cream evenly in chilled crust. Freeze until firm, cut into wedges to serve. Garnish with peach slices or other fresh fruit, if desired.

Melinda Wilkins

Millionaire Pie

3 eggs
1½ C. sugar
¾ stick butter
2 T. vinegar
4 T. water
1 C. raisins
1 C. nuts
¼ t. cinnamon
¼ t. nutmeg
¼ t. allspice
Pinch of salt

Wash raisins and boil 5 minutes in vinegar and water. Beat eggs; cream sugar and butter, add eggs, spices, nuts and raisins. Use what water is left in raisins. Put in unbaked pie crust and bake at 350° for 30–35 minutes. Very rich.

Annie Lee Lasley

Lemon Ice Box Pie

1 can sweetened condensed milk
½ C. lemon juice
1 t. grate lemon rind
2 egg yolks

In medium bowl blend milk, lemon juice, rind, and egg yolks. Stir until thick. Pour into graham cracker or vanilla wafer crust. Cover with meringue, sealing around edges and bake at 325° until brown.

Meringue:

2 egg whites
¼ t. cream of tatar
¼ C. sugar

In small bowl, beat egg whites and cream of tartar to soft peaks. Add sugar gradually and whip to form peaks.

Mrs. Curtis McMillan

Lemon Ice Box Pie

1 can Borden's Eagle Brand Milk
½ C. lemon juice
3 eggs—separated
1 Graham cracker pie crust
2–3 T. sugar

Mix egg yolks with Eagle Brand Milk and lemon juice. Pour into Graham cracker crust. Beat egg whites, gradually adding sugar until forms stiff peaks. Spread over top of pie. Brown in 450° oven.

Rebecca B. Porter

Sunny Silver Pie

⅓ C. water
1 T. gelatin
4 eggs
3 T. lemon juice
½ lemon rind—grated
1 C. sugar
Pinch of salt
1 baked pie shell

Soak gelatin in the ⅓ C. water. Place egg yolks, lemon juice, rind and ½ C. sugar in mixing bowl. Place in large pan of boiling water, keep boiling and whip egg mixture until quite thick and creamy. Turn down heat and fold in gelatin. Beat egg whites very stiff and combine with the other ½ C. sugar. Fold this into yolk mixture. Pour filling in pie shell. Chill in refrigerator for two hours or longer. Serve with whipped cream.

Mrs. Ray Lasley

Innkeeper's Pie

2 squares unsweetened chocolate
   (melted)
⅔ C. oleo
2 C. confectioners sugar
2 eggs (separated)
1 t. vanilla
1 quart "Pralines and Cream" ice
   cream
1¼ C. crushed vanilla wafers,
   divided

Melt chocolate in saucepan; add margarine and sugar. Combine egg yolks and vanilla and add to warm mixture; set aside to cool. Beat egg whites until stiff and add to cooled mixture. Pour mixture on top of 1 cup vanilla wafer crumbs. Freeze 2 hours. Add ice cream. Sprinkle ¼ C. vanilla wafer crumbs on top and freeze.

Nancy Woosley

Beverly's Peppermint Dessert

¾ C. graham cracker crumbs
   (place in bottom of ungreased
   9 x 13 inch dish)
2 squares baking chocolate
⅔ C. margarine
2 C. powdered sugar
2 egg yolks
1 t. vanilla
1 C. chopped pecans
2 egg whites
½ gallon peppermint ice cream,
   softened
¼ C. graham cracker crumbs

Melt chocolate with margarine. Add powdered sugar, egg yolks, vanilla and pecans. Stir in egg whites, stiffly beaten. Put chocolate mixture on top of crumbs. Freeze at least 2 hours. Add ice cream. Spread evenly on top of chocolate layer. Sprinkle ¼ C. crumbs on top. Freeze. Cut in squares to serve. (It's rich).

Beverly Buntin

Country Fried Pies

1 8 oz. pkg. dried fruit (apples,
   peaches, etc.)
1 C. sugar
1 t. apple pie spice
3–4 cans 10-count biscuits

Cover dried fruit with water and cook until tender and not juicy. Add 1 cup sugar and 1 teaspoon apple pie spice. Stir until dissolved. Roll out biscuits 1 at the time on floured board until very thin. Place 1 Tablespoon fruit on ½ of dough. Fold over, forming half-circle shape, and crimp edges with fork. Fry in electric skillet in about 1 inch oil at 350°–400° browning on both sides. Makes 30–40 pies.

Cynthia Grimsley

Apple Pie

1 stick margarine
1¼ C. sugar
1 t. cinnamon
¼ t. salt
1 egg—well beaten
1½ C. chopped apples
1 unbaked pie shell

Mix cinnamon and salt with sugar and add to melted butter. Blend beaten egg and apples and stir into other ingredients. Pour into unbaked pie shell. Bake in 400° oven for 10 minutes, then decrease to 350° until apples are tender.

Annie Lee Lasley

Easy Apple Pie

2 C. grated apples
1½ C. sugar
2 T. flour
1½ t. vanilla
1 egg
¾ stick margarine—melted
½ t. cinnamon
1 unbaked pie shell

Mix well, place in unbaked pie shell. Bake at 350° for 55 minutes. Serves 8–10.

Mrs. Frank Smith

Lemon Lush

1 stick oleo—softened 1 C. flour ½ C. nuts—chopped	Mix and press in 9 x 13 inch pan. Bake 15 minutes in a 350° oven. Let cool.
1¼ C. confectioners sugar 1 8 oz. package cream cheese 1 carton Cool Whip	Mix and spread over crust—refrigerate.
1 large package lemon pudding mix 3 cups milk	Cook pudding mix (regular kind) with milk as directed on package. Cool and spread over mixture above—top with Cool Whip. Refrigerate and serve.

Thelma Kemp

Strawberry Fluff

Crust:

1 C. flour ½ C. chopped nuts ¼ C. brown sugar 1 stick margarine	Combine ingredients for crust in 13 x 9 x 2 inch baking dish. Bake in a 350° oven for 20 minutes, stirring often. Reserve ¼ C. for topping, and spread the rest evenly in the bottom of the pan.

Filling:

1 10 oz. package frozen strawberries 1 C. sugar (⅔ cup sugar, if berries are sweetened) 2 egg whites 2 T. lemon juice 1 10 oz. package frozen whipped topping	Meanwhile, mix frozen berries, sugar, egg whites and lemon juice at high speed in mixer until light and foamy. Fold in thawed topping. Sprinkle reserved crumbs on top; freeze overnight. Remove 15 minutes before serving. Cut into squares. Serves 12-15 people.

Eleanor Haskins

Foolproof Pie Crust

4 C. all purpose flour
1¾ C. Crisco shortening
1 T. sugar
2 t. salt
1 T. vinegar
1 lg. egg
½ C. water

With fork, mix together first 4 ingredients. In a separate dish, mix and beat remaining ingredients. Combine the two mixtures with a fork until all are moistened. Then with hands, mold dough into a ball. Chill 30 minutes before roling into desired shape. Dough can be left in refrigerator up to 3 days; or roll dough, place in pie pans and freeze until ready to use. Thaw 30–40 minutes before baking pie shells. Bake 15 minutes at 425°. The recipe makes 5 9-inch pie shells.

Ethelyn Barlow

Date Pudding

1 C. chopped pecans
1 C. chopped dates
1 T. flour
1 T. baking powder
3 eggs—separated
1 C. sugar

Sift flour and baking powder over nuts and dates. Separate eggs. Add sugar slowly to beaten egg yolks. Add to nut mixture. Beat whites to form stiff peaks, then fold into egg mixture. Pour into well-greased 10 x 13 inch pan; bake 45 minutes at 350°. Turn off oven, open oven door, and let set 10–15 minutes. Cool on wire rack.

Mrs. L. P. Jackson

Sweet Potato Pudding

3 C. sweet potatoes—grated
1 C. milk
1½ C. sugar
3 eggs—beaten
½ C. butter—melted
1 t. nutmeg
½ t. allspice
2 t. cinnamon

Grate potatoes. Add to milk. Add sugar, beaten eggs, butter and spices. Mix well. Bake in well-greased skillet in a 325° oven for 1 hour or until brown and firm.

Anne L. Shaw

Desserts

Uncooked Banana Pudding

2 boxes (3¾ oz.) instant vanilla
   pudding
3 C. cold milk
16 oz. carton Cool Whip
1 can Eagle Brand Milk
Bananas
Vanilla Wafers

Mix pudding with cold milk, beat until thick. Add Eagle Brand Milk slowly. Spoon in Cool Whip. Layer with wafers and bananas. Makes large bowl.

Katherine Goodson

Lemon Pudding

1 C. sugar
2 t. grated lemon rind
¼ t. salt
⅓ C. sifted flour
2 T. butter—melted
3 T. lemon juice
3 eggs—separated
1½ C. sweet milk

Mix together sugar, salt, lemon juice and rind, add egg yolks and beat well. Add flour, mixing well; blend in melted butter and milk. Beat egg whites until stiff and fold into egg mixture. Pour into greased, 2-quart casserole dish. Set in pan of hot water and bake in moderate oven (350°) 45–50 minutes.

Annie Lee Lasley

Peach Crumble

6–8 medium peaches
¼ C. brown sugar
½ c. flour
⅛ t. nutmeg
¼ C. butter

Peel peaches, slice, arrange around edge of Pyrex dish. Mix dry ingredients; add butter and mix with pastry blender. Put sugar mixture over peaches. Bake at 350° for 25–30 minutes.

Judy Haskins

Easy Cobbler

1 stick margarine
1 C. sugar
1 C. all purpose flour
¾ C. milk
2 t. baking powder
2 cans fruit or 2–4 cups fresh fruit

Melt margarine in a casserole dish. Mix sugar, flour, milk and baking powder and pour on butter. Don't mix. Put fruit on top. Cover top generously with sugar and cinnamon. Bake at 350°. Serves 8–10.

Leigh Geyer

Desserts

Easy Country Cobbler

1 stick butter
1 C. self-rising flour
1 C. sugar
1 C. milk
1 can fruit (drained or fresh)

Melt butter in 1½ quart or 2 quart casserole dish. Mix flour, sugar and milk in bowl. Pour fruit into butter; pour flour mixture over fruit. Place in 350° oven for 45–50 minutes.

Karen Bundy

Frosty Fruit Dessert

2 C. sugar
⅛ t. salt
1 quart (4 C.) buttermilk
1 t. vanilla
20 oz. can crushed pineapple—drained
17 oz. can fruit cocktail—drained

Combine drained fruit juices with buttermilk to make 4 cups. Store remaining buttermilk in refrigerator. In large bowl combine sugar, salt, buttermilk and vanilla until well mixed. Gently stir in drained fruits. Pour into a 9 inch square pan. Freeze until firm, but not hard. Serves 8–12. Store remainder in freezer or refrigerator.

Gloria Gardner

Oreo Cookies Dessert

3 rows (approx. 3 doz.) Oreo cookies (crushed)
1 regular size can Hershey's syrup
6 Heath bars (crushed)
½ gallon vanilla ice cream (softened)

Mix first 3 ingredients. Grease 13 x 6 inch pan or pyrex dish with butter, spread ½ mixture in pan and freeze. Spread ½ gallon ice cream and top with remaining mixture and return to freezer. Cut and top with whipped cream (optional).

Leigh Ann Jones Taylor

Miscellaneous

Smoke House Pickles
(Old Recipe)

16 lbs. cucumbers
10 lbs. sugar
1 box pickling spices
½ box alum
1 gallon vinegar
2 C. pickling salt
1 gallon water or enough to cover
    cucumbers

Soak whole cucumbers in salt water mixture (brine) for 14 days (8 days if sliced). Pour off salt water and slice if you left whole at first. Soak in alum water to cover for 8 hours or overnight. Wash and drain. Soak in gallon of vinegar overnight. Drain vinegar. Put layer of cucumbers and layer of sugar in large crock until all of 10 lbs. of sugar is used. Put spices in a cloth and put in crock. Pour vinegar back over cucumbers. Will keep in crock indefinitely.

Mrs. Lester Mangold

Peach Pickle

5 lbs. peaches
3 lbs. sugar
1 quart vinegar
Cloves

Let peaches and sugar, with very little water, come to a boil. Add vinegar and cloves (tied in thin cloth). Let peaches cook until tender. Remove when tender into sterilized jars. Let the syrup come to a boil until very thick. Pour syrup over peaches and seal.

Mrs. Ray Lasley

Pickled Peaches

5 lbs. peaches (fully ripe)
4 C. sugar
2 C. vinegar
1 C. water
1 T. cloves
1 T. Allspice
4–6 2" sticks cinnamon

Peel peaches and pack in jars with 1 stick cinnamon in each jar. Pour in hot syrup. Process jars of peaches in hot water bath 10 minutes. Let ripen 6 weeks.

Cynthia Grimsley

Watermelon Rind Pickle

Watermelon rind
1 T. pickling lime
1 quart water
7 C. sugar
2 C. white vinegar
¼ t. oil of clove
½ t. oil of cinnamon
Red or green food coloring
   (optional)

Peel and cut the watermelon rind into 1-inch cubes. Soak, covered in lime and water mixture for 2 hours or over night. Wash well and drain. Cover watermelon with water and bring to boil, uncovered. Cook until transparent or until tender (about 30 minutes). Drain. Bring last 5 ingredients to boil to make syrup and cook about 10 minutes. Pour over rinds. Put in sterile jars and seal.

Imogene Tisdale

Pickled Okra

3½ lbs. small okra pods
1 pint white vinegar
1 quart water
⅓ C. salt
3 small hot peppers (optional)
2 t. dill seed
1 garlic bud per pint jar

Pack okra firmly in jars. Put garlic bud in each jar. Pour boiling brine over okra in jars and seal. Process in boiling water bath 10 minutes.

Cynthia Grimsley

Freezer Cucumbers

7 cucumbers—sliced with peeling
   on
3 onions—sliced thin
1 bell pepper—sliced round
2 C. sugar
1 C. vinegar
1 T. canning salt
½ t. celery seed

Stir together last 4 ingredients. Pour over sliced cucumbers, onions, and pepper. Put in containers and freeze.

Georgie Mallard

Freezer Pickles

8 C. thinly sliced cucumbers
1 large onion—sliced
1½ T. salt
1½ C. sugar
½ C. vinegar

Mix cucumbers and onions and sprinkle with salt, let set 2 hours; pour off liquid. Mix sugar with vinegar and pour over cucumbers and onions. Let set 10 minutes, put in freezer boxes and freeze.

Cynthia Grimsley

Red Hot Pickle Rings

2 gallons cucumbers
2 C. lime
8½ quarts water
1 C. vinegar
1 small bottle red food coloring
1 T. alum
3½ C. water
3½ C. vinegar
10 C. sugar
3 packages Cinnamon Red Hots
8 sticks cinnamon
1 C. sugar

Slice cucumbers and remove all seeds from center. Soak in solution of 2 C. lime and 8½ quarts water for 24 hours, stirring occasionally. Remove and rinse 3 times. Put in ice water. Mix 1 C. vinegar, red food coloring, and 1 T. alum; simmer. Add cucumber rings. Add enough water to completely cover. Simmer 2 hours. Drain and discard liquid. Mix 3½ C. water, 3½ C. vinegar, 10 C. sugar, red hots, and cinnamon. Bring to a boil and pour over drained rings. Save liquid each time. Let stand 24 hours. Drain mixture from cucumbers, add 1 C. sugar, and bring to a boil. Pour over rings; let stand 24 hours. Drain liquid from cucumbers, again bringing to a boil, and pouring over rings. Bring the whole mixture (liquid and rings) to a boil. Put in hot sterilized jars and seal.

Jana Childress

Ripe Tomato Relish

1 gallon ripe tomatoes
1 pint onions
1 quart vinegar
1 quart sugar
¼ C. hot pepper
1 t. black pepper
1 T. salt
4 green bell peppers

Finely chop all vegetables, mixing well. Cook on medium heat until thick, stirring frequently. Seal in sterilized jars.

Sarah Lasley Ralls

Uncooked Ripe Relish

1 peck ripe tomatoes
4 stalks celery
6 medium onions
6 green peppers
½ C. salt
3 lbs. brown sugar
3 oz. white mustard seed
1 quart vinegar
1 t. cinnamon

Grind and drain tomatoes in bag overnight. Next morning, grind peppers and add to tomatoes. Mix all ingredients well and place in crock; cover for protection, but do not seal.

Mrs. Ray Lasley

Strawberry Freezer Jam

1 package powdered pectin
1 C. water
3½ C. mashed fresh strawberries
5 C. sugar

In a large saucepan, combine pectin and water and bring to a boil. Boil one minute. Stir in strawberries and sugar and boil 1 minute longer. Refrigerate overnight before packaging for freezer. Makes about 4 cups jam. Freeze in small plastic containers.

Kay Shaw Cobb

Ice Cream/Custard

1 quart milk
3 eggs—well beaten
1 C. sugar
9 large marshmallows
1 t. vanilla

On low heat, cook until mixture forms a coating on spoon. Freeze, using fruit if desired. This can also be used as boiled custard.

Jackson Mayor Bob Conger

Junket Ice Cream

½ gallon milk
2½ C. sugar
1 t. vanilla flavoring
1 large can Carnation milk
2 Junket tablets
Fruit (optional)

Heat the milk to lukewarm temperature. Dissolve sugar in milk and flavor with a little vanilla. Dissolve two Junket tablets and, when melted, add to milk. Pour into freezer container and let the mixture clabber. After it has clabbered, pour in one large can of Carnation milk. The last ingredient to add is your fruit if you want fruit ice cream. You are now ready to freeze.

Norma Wilson

Ice Cream

4 eggs
2½ C. sugar
7 C. milk
3 C. whipping cream
2½ T. vanilla
½ T. salt

Whip eggs until fluffy. Add sugar gradually. Add remaining ingredients. Freeze in ice cream freezer. Makes one gallon.

Kay Henson

Traditional Boiled Custard from Bells, Tenn.

3 pints sweet milk
1 T. flour
1 C. sugar
4 eggs

Put milk in the top of a double boiler and bring almost to a boil. Sift together 2 times the dry ingredients. Beat eggs with a rotary beater. Combine with dry mixture until well mixed but do not over-beat. Combine egg and sugar mixture with hot milk. Stir constantly. When done, the custard will coat the spoon. When the custard is very cold, add ½ t. pure vanilla. Top each serving with whipped cream and a cherry.

Beverly Buntin

Microwave Boiled Custard

1 quart milk
5 eggs
1 C. sugar
1 t. vanilla

Place milk in microwave for 3 minutes on high. Stir. Beat eggs together until light, add sugar to eggs and mix well. Pour a small portion of hot milk into egg and sugar mixture to warm and thin this portion. Pour slowly into hot milk. Return to microwave for 3 minutes on high. Stir. Return to microwave for 2 minutes on high. Stir. Return to microwave for 2 more minutes on high. Stir. Continue in 30 second intervals stirring after each segment until coats spoon (I cooked for 11 minutes). Do not boil. Add vanilla.

Leigh Ann Jones

Pineapple Sherbert
(Very old recipe)

1 quart water
3 C. sugar
6 lemons
1 large can crushed pineapple

Make lemonade with water, sugar and lemons. Add pineapple. Freeze until it is a mush. Add rich milk to fill one gallon ice cream freezer.

Eleanor Lasley Haskins

Heavenly Fruit Dip

½ C. sugar
2 T. all-purpose flour
1 C. pineapple juice
1 egg—beaten
1 T. margarine
1 C. whipping cream—whipped

Combine first 5 ingredients in a heavy saucepan. Cook over medium heat, stirring constantly, until smooth and thickened. Let cool completely. Fold in whipped cream. Makes about 2 cups.

Barbara Higgs

Rick's Ro-Tel Dip

1 lb. Velveeta Cheese
1 can Ro-Tel
½ lb. mild country sausage

Drain juice from Ro-Tel and mash. Put cheese in top of double boiler— melt. Fry sausage and crumble. Mix Ro-Tel and cheese together, add sausage. Keep hot in chafing dish and serve with choice of chips.

T. Clark Shaw

Ro-Tel Cheese Dip

1 lb. ground beef
1 lb. American cheese
¼ t. chili powder
1 8 oz. can Ro-Tel tomatoes and
  chile peppers
2 T. Worchestershire sauce

Brown ground beef; drain. Melt cheese into ground beef; add other ingredients. Serve warm. Delicious with Fritos corn chips or served over slice of party rye bread.

Katharine Goodson

Spinach Dip

1 C. sour cream
1 C. Hellman's mayonnaise
1 package Knorr Swiss vegetable
  soup mix
1 package frozen spinach—cooked
  and drained
1 C. water chestnuts—chopped
3 green onions—tops and bottoms

Mix and chill for 3 hours. Great with Wheat Thins or Triscuits!!

Kelley Walker

Vegetable Dip

1½ C. sour cream
2½ C. mayonnaise
1 C. finely chopped onion
2 t. salt
¼ t. Tabasco sauce
1 C. chopped bell pepper
½ C. finely chopped pimento
½ t. pepper
¼ t. garlic salt

Combine all ingredients, cover and chill at least 1 hour. Better if chilled over night. Serve with fresh carrot sticks, celery, broccoli, cauliflower, etc. Makes 5 cups.

Diane Cathey

Cheese Puffs

2 C. mild cheddar cheese—grated
½ C. butter or oleo
1 C. flour
½ t. salt
1 t. paprika
Olives

Mix all ingredients together except olives. Roll dough into walnut size balls around olives. Bake at 400° for 15 minutes. May be frozen and cooked at last minute. Serve hot. Makes 48 balls.

Norma Taylor

Cheese Ball

1 8 oz. package Philadelphia Cream
    Cheese
1 sm. jar olives
1 package pecans—crushed

Cheese should be room temperature. Chop olives finely. Mix olives and cheese well. Shape into ball and roll in chopped pecans. Serves 15.

Donna Davis

Cheese Straws

½ lb. cheddar cheese—grated
½ lb. oleo (2 sticks)
½ lb. flour (2 C.)

Let cheese and oleo come to room temperature, then combine. Add flour and make into small rolls. Chill, slice, and cook at 400° for 15 minutes.

Sausage Tidbits

3 C. Bisquick
1 lb. hot sausage
1 10 oz. package sharp cheddar
    cheese

Have sausage at room temperature. Mix thoroughly all ingredients and roll in little balls. Place on ungreased cookie sheet and bake at 400° for 15 to 18 minutes or until golden brown.

Kay Henson

Peter Piper Sandwiches

4 slices buttered bread
4 sweet gherkins
4 slices American cheese
2 strips bacon

Toast bread on one side; arrange on broiler pan. Slice pickle; put on toast; add slices of cheese on pickle. Cut bacon fine and put on cheese. Broil about 2 minutes.

Anne L. Shaw

Apricot Spiced Punch

3 C. apricot nectar
3 C. apple cider
1 C. water
3 T. sugar
3 T. lemon juice
8 whole cloves
7 4" cinnamon sticks

Combine first 6 ingredients in a 3-quart saucepan; bring to a boil, stirring until sugar is dissolved. Remove from heat; let stand about 2 hours to improve flavor. Reheat before serving. Serve with cinnamon sticks, if desired. Makes 7 cups.

Betty Cole Lufkin

Spiced Tea

3 quarts boiling water
6 tea bags
1½ C. sugar
½ C. lemon juice
1½ C. orange juice
1 C. boiling water
1 t. whole cloves
1 t. whole allspice
1" stick cinnamon

Add cloves, allspice, and cinnamon to 1 C. boiling water. Let simmer 5 minutes and strain. Let tea bags steep in 3 quarts boiling water 5 minutes; then add sugar, lemon juice, orange juice and the 1 C. of spiced water.

Annie Lee Lasley

Punch

4 cans pineapple juice
4 cans frozen lemonade—made up
8 packages lemon-lime Kool-Aid
2½ quarts water
5 C. sugar

Very large recipe. Can be cut in half. Serve chilled.

J. Lawrence Taylor

Fruit Punch

1 package strawberry jello
2 C. boiling water
1½ C. sugar
1½ C. pineapple juice
1 C. lemon juice
8–10 C. water
1 tub pineapple sherbert

Mix jello and water. Add remaining liquid ingredients and pour over sherbert. Fills one punch bowl.

Leigh Geyer

Punch

4½ C. sugar
4½ C. water
2 pints orange juice—frozen if desired
1 lg. can pineapple juice
Juice of 1 dozen lemons
2 quarts ginger ale
½ gallon orange sherbert

Boil together sugar and water. Mix with remaining ingredients except ale and sherbert. Chill. When ready to serve, pour ginger ale over sherbert. Then pour remaining ingredients. The juices and water make 1 gallon.

Kay Henson

Holiday Punch

1 quart boiling water
15 small teabags
1 t. whole cloves
1 6 oz. can lemonade
2 C. cranberry juice
1 20 oz. can crushed pineapple
2 C. orange juice
Sugar to taste
Lemon slices
Cinnamon sticks (optional)

Pour boiling water over tea and cloves. Brew 4 minutes. Stir and strain. Add remaining ingredients except lemon slices and cinnamon sticks. Pour into pre-heated bowl. Garnish with clove-studded lemon slices. If desired, place a cinnamon stick in each punch cup to serve as a muddler.

Microwave 2-Minute Fudge

1 box powdered sugar
½ C. cocoa
1 stick margarine
¼ C. milk
1 C. chopped nuts
1 T. vanilla

Put sugar, cocoa, and margarine in microwave dish, put in microwave oven for 2 minutes on high. Stir, then add milk, nuts, and vanilla. Pour in greased pyrex dish and refrigerate.

Donna Hewitt

Sour Cream Fudge

2 C. granulated sugar
½ t. salt
1 8 oz. carton sour cream
1 cup nuts (optional)
1 lump of butter (about the size of half an egg)

Mix sugar, salt, and sour cream thoroughly and place on low heat, stirring constantly. When candy forms a ball in cold water which can be picked up with fingers, remove from heat very carefully. Add nuts now, if desired. Let stand about 30 minutes, but do not stir until after 30 minutes. Then begin beating and do so until it begins to thicken. Lift large spoons full of fudge onto buttered pan. Pat out with back of spoon. Wait a few minutes before cutting into squares.

**Mary Mays Hudson
(91 year old lady piano player at OLD COUNTRY STORE)**

Caramel Candy

½ C. sugar
2 T. butter
2½ C. sugar
1 C. milk
1 t. vanilla

Brown ½ cup sugar and butter together until caramelized. In another saucepan, let 2 C. sugar and milk slowly come to a boil. Add caramelized sugar to milk mixture. Cook until it forms a soft ball in cold water. Add vanilla. Let candy cool; then beat until light and creamy. Pour into a greased dish. Cool a little longer. Cut into small squares.

Margorie Lasley Scott

Peanut Brittle

1½ C. sugar
½ C. white Karo syrup
½ C. water
2 C. shelled peanuts
1½ t. soda
Thimble-sized piece of parafin

Mix together sugar, syrup, water, and parafin, and boil about 10 minutes, stirring often. Remove from heat, beat in soda and peanuts. Quickly pour onto greased cookie sheet. Cool and break into pieces.

Evelyn Smith

Apricot Candy Roll

3 C. sugar
1 C. evaporated milk
1 C. dried apricots—finely chopped
¼ C. butter (½ butter)
½ t. salt
2 t. vanilla
½ C. nuts—finely chopped

Combine sugar, evaporated milk, apricots, butter and salt in saucepan; stirring constantly. Bring to a boil. Boil, stirring occasionally, to the soft ball stage (236°). Cool to lukewarm (120°). Add vanilla and nuts, beat until stiff enough to knead. Place on bread board and knead until smooth. Shape into 4 small rolls about an inch in diameter. Place in refrigerator to chill for several hours. Cut into small slices. Makes about 80 small pieces.

Marjorie Lasley Scott

Fruit Nut Roll

2 C. chopped pecans
1 sm. jar cherries
½ box raisins (optional)
1 can Eagle Brand Milk
1 can Angel Flake Coconut
1 lg. bag vanilla wafers

Crumble wafers fine; stir into milk, add raisins, cherries, and pecans. Mix well with hands. Sprinkle aluminum foil with coconut. Lay mixture on foil. Form roll and wrap in foil. Store in refrigerator for 1 day, then slice.

Sharon Deaton

Miscellaneous

Party Log

1 box vanilla wafers—crushed
2 C. pecans—chopped
2 C. miniature marshmallows
1 can Eagle Brand Milk
1½ C. raisins or dates
½ C. Maraschino cherries—
　　chopped
½ C. confectioners sugar

Mix all ingredients together. Shape into logs. Roll in confectioners sugar.

Strawberry Candy

2 packages family-size strawberry
　　jello
1 7 oz. can coconut
1 can Eagle Brand Milk
Red candied sugar

Mix jello and coconut, add milk and mix. Chill. Shape into balls and roll in candied sugar. Dye almonds green and stick in candy for stems.

Sharon Deaton

Lemon Sauce
(Very Old Recipe)

1 egg—well beaten
1 C. sugar
3 T. boiling water
Juice of 1 lemon
Grated lemon rind
1 T. butter

Cook in double boiler until slightly thickened

Annie Lee Lasley

Butter Sauce for Desserts

2 egg yolks
⅓ C. sugar
⅓ C. butter—melted
2 T. lemon juice
1 T. grated lemon rind
⅓ C. whipped cream

Beat egg yolks until thick and lemon colored, gradually add sugar, continually beating. Add butter, lemon juice, and rind. Fold in whipped cream. Chill. Delicious on gingerbread.

Miscellaneous

Bar-B-Que Sauce

1½ gallons vinegar
2 C. salt
2 C. Worcestershire sauce
1½ C. Tabasco sauce

Bring ingredients to a boil. Baste chicken, pork, or beef. Especially good on chicken.

Norwood Jones

Cucumber Dressing

1 quart Kraft mayonnaise
3 medium cucumbers
3 small onions
¼ C. lemon juice
¼ C. sugar
¼ t. green food coloring
¼ t. garlic powder
2 T. Worcestershire sauce

Grind cucumbers and onions in blender. DRAIN WELL. Add sugar, lemon juice, and other seasonings. Add color. Add mayonnaise and stir until smooth. Chill. Keeps well in the refrigerator.

Beverly Buntin

Swiss Asparagus Casserole

1 large can cut asparagus
4 T. butter or oleo
3 T. flour
1½ C. milk
1 can mushroom soup
1 t. pimentos
3 hard boiled eggs
½ t. salt
¼ t. paprika
2 C. bread crumbs mixed with
   melted butter or oleo
½ lb. cooking cheese
2 T. chopped celery
1 T. chopped onion

Melt butter. Add salt, paprika and flour. Cook and stir until smooth. Stir in milk and continue cooking until sauce is thick. Add mushroom soup and cheese cut in small pieces and stir until melted. Add celery and pimentos. Add onion which has been sauteed in butter. Place a layer of asparagus and then eggs and another layer of asparagus. Pour sauce over all. Top with bread crumbs. Bake 20 minutes or until browned at 300°.

Maxine Crumby

Cheese Casserole

1 large carton of cottage cheese
8 to 12 oz. grated cheddar cheese
1 lb. Velveeta cheese, cubed
¾ stick of margarine, cubed
4 eggs

Combine ingredients and place in glass dish. Cook at 350° for 30-40 minutes or until bubbly and beginning to brown. Set out for 10 minutes before serving.

Gloria J. Roberts

Escalloped Pineapple

3 eggs
2 C. sugar
½ lb. butter (2 sticks)
1 #2 can crushed pineapple
    (juice and all)
4 C. bread cubes

Mix eggs, sugar and butter (melted) together. Blend in pineapple and bread cubes. Bake in a 350° oven for 30 minutes. Serves 10 to 12 people.

Wanda Fowler

Pineapple Casserole

2 (20 oz.) cans chunk pineapple
¾ C. sugar
6 T. flour
2 C. grated cheddar cheese
½ C. melted butter
1 C. Ritz cracker crumbs

Drain pineapple, reserving 6 T. of juice. Combine sugar and flour, stir in juice. Add melted butter, cheese and pineapple. Pour into 2 quart casserole. Bake in a 350° oven for 20 minutes. Add crumbs and reduce heat—cook for 20-30 minutes or until golden brown.

Norma Taylor

Shaw's Potato Casserole

5 to 6 medium to large potatoes—
   sliced
1 onion, chopped
6 strips of bacon, fried and crumbled
2 C. of shredded cheddar cheese
1 stick of butter or margarine, melted
Salt and pepper

Grease a 9 x 13 inch pyrex dish. Arrange this recipe in layers beginning with a single layer of potatoes, sprinkle chopped onion, crumbled bacon and shredded cheese. Pour enough butter or margarine just to coat top and salt and pepper to taste. Repeat layers until you run out of ingredients. Cover top with any remaining cheese. Cover pyrex dish with aluminum foil. Bake in a 400° oven for 1 hour.

Juanita Shaw

Tomato Casserole

1 can stewed tomatoes
1 8 oz. package Mozzarella cheese
   (cubed)
3 pieces of toast (cubed)
1 medium onion (grated)
1 t. pepper
¼ C. melted butter

Saute onion in butter. Mix and put in casserole. Save 2 slices of Mozzarella cheese to garnish top. Bake 20 minutes at 375°.

Nancy Wooley

Fried Potato Cakes

4 C. mashed potatoes
1 egg
¼ C sour cream
1½ T. chopped parsley (optional)
3 green onions, chopped
Flour
Bacon drippings

Beat potatoes, egg and sour cream. Add parsley and green onions. Shape into patties and sprinkle with flour. Fry in hot bacon fat or oil until crusty and brown.

Thelma Kemp

Cheese-It Cups

1 16 oz. can pork n' beans
2 wieners, sliced penny style
¼ C. barbecue sauce
1 T. brown sugar
1 t. minced onion
½ C. shredded cheddar cheese
1 (10 count) can biscuits

Place one biscuit in muffin tin, pressing sides. Fill each cup with mixture of first 5 ingredients. Sprinkle with cheese. Bake 10-15 minutes in a 425° oven.

Sandra Magee

Natchez Eggs

6 eggs
2 T. half-n-half
6 T. grated cheddar cheese
Salt and pepper

Grease muffin tins with margarine. Break eggs into each individual tin. Add 1 t. half-n-half to each egg. Add 1 T. grated cheese to top egg. Bake in a 350° oven for 10 to 15 minutes, depending on how done you like your eggs. Loosen edges with knife and use a spoon for easy lifting of egg.

Juanita Shaw

Cheese Ball

1 lb. cottage cheese
2 8 oz. packages cream cheese
1 lb. sharp cheddar cheese (grated)
1 medium onion (grated)
2 T. salad dressing
1 small jar chopped olives
1 small jar chopped pimento
Garlic powder
Red pepper
Chopped pecans
Paprika

Mix together and chill. Roll ball in chopped pecans mixed with paprika.

Margaret Hewitt

Hot Chicken Salad

2 C. cooked chicken, cut in chunks
2 C. chopped celery
3 T. minced onions
3 T. lemon juice
½ t. salt
½ t. black pepper
½ C. pecans
¾ C. mayonnaise
1 C. sliced mushrooms
1 can cream of chicken soup
Potato chips

Mix all ingredients except the soup and potato chips. Place in 2 quart casserole. Pour soup over top without mixing. Top with crushed potato chips and bake in a 300° oven for 30 minutes. Serves 6-8 people.

Louise Dent

Egg Casserole Breakfast

14-16 slices of white bread (trimmed)
16 slices of ham (broken up)
7-8 slices Swiss cheese
14-16 slices American cheese
3 C. milk
6 eggs
2 cups corn flakes, crushed
½ C. oleo, melted

Beat together milk and eggs. Add salt and pepper.

Trim bread, cut into sections. Put one layer in bottom of pan.

In a 9 x 13 inch buttered pan, layer bread, cheese, ham, milk and egg mixture. Make two layers.

Mix together crushed corn flakes and melted oleo. Place over casserole. Bake in a 400° oven for approximately 25 minutes.

*Note—I use 2-3 C. milk, ½ t. salt and 1 t. pepper.

Sue Woods

Sweet and Sour Beans

10 strips bacon
1 medium onion, diced
1 C. vinegar
1 C. sugar
4 16 oz. cans French-style green
    beans, drained

Fry bacon. Crumble. Saute onion in a little bacon grease. Mix all ingredients. Chill. Heat thoroughly and drain.

Becky Cargile

Favorites

BROOKS SHAW & SON

THE OLD COUNTRY STORE

Old Country Store Orange Dressing

1 medium Cool Whip
1 small package vanilla instant
 pudding mix
1 C. milk
2 t. orange extract

Mix as directed on box of pudding, adding extract. Fold into Cool Whip and chill. Serve on fresh fruit.

Old Country Store Restaurant

Old Country Store Fruit Punch

1 large can unsweetened
 pineapple juice
1 small can frozen lemonade
½ C. sugar
2 bottles ginger ale

Freeze pineapple juice 3–4 hours before serving. Needs to be a slush. Mix frozen lemonade and sugar. Add pineapple juice. Add ginger ale last.

Old Country Store Restaurant

Old Country Store Fried Green Tomatoes

2 green tomatoes (sliced ½″ thick
 slices)
4 eggs, beaten
1 cup corn meal
¼ cup flour
1 teaspoon salt
1 dash black pepper

Mix all dry ingredients thoroughly. Dredge tomatoes in egg. Dust with corn meal mix. Fry in 350° oil until golden brown on both sides. Serves 2.

Old Country Store Restaurant

Old Country Store Baked Beans
For a Big Bean Party

6 cans (#10) pork and beans
1 16 oz. box brown sugar
28 oz. ketchup
3 large onions diced
3 large green peppers diced
1 lb. pulled barbecue

Mix all ingredients together. Bake in 350° oven for 1½ hours. Serves 125–130.

Old Country Store Restaurant

Old Country Store Corn Pudding

6 large cans cream corn
1 C. margarine
12 eggs—beaten
1½ C. sugar
1 t. black pepper
1 t. salt
3½ C. sweet milk
4 C. flour

Mix all ingredients together except milk and flour. Measure milk and flour and mix together well. Add to corn and mix well. Bake at 350° for 45–60 minutes. Serves 110-150 people.

Old Country Store Restaurant

Old Country Store Cole Slaw

1 medium head green cabbage
(shredded to ⅛")
1 carrot (shredded)

Dressing:

2 C. mayonnaise
¼ C. white vinegar
¾ C. sugar
2 T. milk

Mix all dressing ingredients together thoroughly in a large bowl until smooth.

Add cabbage and carrots. Mix until evenly coated. Refrigerate until ready to serve. Serves 8–10.

Old Country Store Restaurant

Old Country Store Seafood and Pasta Salad

1 lb. cooked macaroni
4 oz. seafood flakes
¾ cup mayonnaise
¼ cup chopped green onion
½ teaspoon salt
Dash black pepper
¼ teaspoon sugar

Mix all of the above ingredients. Allow to refrigerate for two hours before serving. Serves 8–10.

Old Country Store Restaurant

Old Country Store Chess Pie

1½ C. sugar
1½ T. flour
1½ T. meal
1 t. vinegar
¼ C. milk
3 eggs
1 stick butter—melted
1 t. vanilla

Beat eggs. Add sugar, flour, and meal to eggs. Stir. Add vanilla, vinegar, and milk. Lastly, add the melted butter. Stir all ingredients well. Put into unbaked pie shell. Bake at 350° for 45–50 minutes until firm in the middle.

Old Country Store Restaurant

Old Country Store Southern Pecan Pie

3 cups dark brown sugar
3 cups corn syrup (white)
3 teaspoon vanilla
1 cup melted margarine
9 eggs (beaten separately)
3 10-inch pie shells (uncooked)
3 cups pecan pieces

Mix sugar, corn syrup, vanilla and margarine. Add beaten eggs. Fold well. Pour evenly into uncooked pie shells. Top pies with pecan pieces. Bake at 325° for 50 minutes. Makes 3 pies.

Old Country Store Restaurant

Old Country Store Chocolate Chess Pie

1½ C. sugar
3½ T. cocoa
½ stick oleo—melted
2 eggs—beaten
⅔ C. evaporated milk
1 t. vanilla
½ C. pecans (optional)

Mix all ingredients and put in unbaked pie shell. Bake 40–45 minutes at 350°.

Old Country Store Restaurant

CASEY JONES — HIS STORY

HIS FAVORITE PIE AND MRS. JONES' CARROT RELISH

Casey Jones was born Jonathan Luther Jones, March 14, 1863, in Southeast Missouri. His parents moved to Cayce, Kentucky, while he was very young and he later gained his famous nickname by fellow railroaders because of his hometown of Cayce, Kentucky. He grew up along the Mobile & Ohio Railroad and dreamed of becoming an engineer. When he was fifteen, he went to work for the M & O as an apprentice telegrapher. Three years later, he advanced to become a locomotive fireman.

His rendezvous with destiny and the role Jackson, Tennessee, played in his story began in 1884 when he arrived in Jackson to take a flagman's job with the Illinois Central Railroad.

Casey became known as a "fast roller." But the record does not show that he was careless. At a time of keen competition between railroads, every effort was made to reduce schedules in order to attract and keep lucrative mail contracts. Casey had what it took to "get her in on the advertised," and that was what he was doing on the legendary ride between Memphis, Tennessee, and Canton, Mississippi, April 30, 1900.

His final hours began April 29 1900, when he rolled into Memphis on his new Rogers ten-wheeler, No. 382, with his black fireman, Sim Webb. They were told the engineer scheduled to go south to Canton, Mississippi, was ill. Casey said he would do the job if he could have No. 382 and Sim as his fireman.

He had a 190-mile journey ahead and the night was murky. As he neared the little town of Vaughn, Mississippi, the speeding Cannonball came upon red rear marker lights on the main track ahead. A caboose and three railcars were stuck on the track due to a ruptured air hose.

Casey yelled for Sim to "Jump!" and began slowing the train down. In the final seconds of his life, Casey shut down the throttle, threw on the emergency brakes and slammed the gears into reverse. While the locomotive left the track in the wreck, the passenger cars remained on the rails and only Casey was killed.

A black enginewiper at the Canton Roundhouse, Wallace Saunders, composed a ballad about Casey. That ballad is how the world knows about Casey Jones.

Mince Meat Pie
Casey Jones' Favorite

1 cooked pastry shell
1 package mince meat (9 oz.)
1½ C. water
2 T. butter
3 egg yolks
½ C. sugar
1 t. vanilla

Meringue:
3 egg whites—beaten
6 T. sugar

Soak mince meat in water. Add beaten egg yolks and sugar. Cook over hot water until thick, stir in butter and vanilla. Pour in cooked pastry shell and cover with meringue made from egg whites. Spread well over pie. Cook 325° for 12–18 minutes.

Mrs. Casey Jones
As given to Mrs. Guy McMaster

Uncooked Carrot Relish

12 carrots
4 onions
6 green peppers
6 sweet peppers (ripe red)
6 C. sugar
1 C. salt
Vinegar

Wash peppers and carrots. Do not peel. Grind peppers, carrots, and onions. Place in a large pan. Pour salt over this mixture and let stand for several hours. Wash salt out and put sugar and enough vinegar to cover vegetables. Stir at intervals for a few hours. Put in sterilized jars and seal.

Mrs. Casey Jones
As given to Mrs. Guy McMaster

Index

Index

Index

Index

Index

Index

COLLECTIBLES CORNER

Located in our Old Country Store Gift Shoppe is the "Collectibles Corner," filled with some of the highest quality and most popular collectibles you find anywhere, including:

Austin Sculptures

Miss Martha's All God's Children

Bradford Exchange GWTW Plates

Colonial Village by Lefton

Country Champions

Emmitt Kelly Jr.

Monfort

Precious Moments

Tom Clark Gnomes

Cherished Teddies

Wee Forest Folks

Waco Melody in Motion

Rod Mench Civil War Figurines

Call us at (800) 748-9588
if we can assist you with one.

See the following page for popular
Old Country Store gift selections
you may order at home!

Mail Order

POPULAR GIFT SELECTIONS
YOU CAN ORDER AT HOME

Make a memory for someone special with some of the most unique and popular selections from our 6,000 square foot Gift, Confectionery, Collectibles and Souvenir Shoppe. Ordering is easy, quick and convenient.

Number Ordered	Description	Price Each	TN Residents Sales Tax	Shipping & Handling	Totals
_____	Tennessee Gift Basket	$23.99	$2.10	$8.00	_____
_____	Tennessee Breakfast Basket	29.99	2.62	8.00	_____
_____	1 lb. Homemade Fudge: Chocolate, Vanilla, Peanut Butter (nuts optional)	6.99	.61	4.00	
_____	Old Country Store Red Coffee Mugs (Insulated to keep coffee hot)	5.99	.52	4.00	_____
_____	Casey Jones Village Railroad Hat S–M–L–XL	8.99	.79	4.00	_____
_____	Casey Jones Village Railroad Bear	12.99	1.14	4.00	_____
_____	Casey Jones Village T-Shirt	14.99	1.31	4.00	_____
_____	Coon Skin Cap	8.99	.79	4.00	_____
_____	Train Whistle	5.99	.52	4.00	_____
_____	Dixie Door Chime	16.99	1.49	4.00	_____
_____	1 lb. Old Fashioned Marbles	4.99	.44	4.00	_____
_____	Casey Jones Christmas Ornaments	4.99	.44	4.00	_____

SHIP TO:

Name _____

Address _____

City, State, Zip _____

Phone (_____) _____

Please return this page *along with the Merchandise Order Form on the following page* to help us process your order promptly and accurately.

Order Form

COOKBOOK ORDER FORM

You may order additional copies of **The Old Country Store Cookbook** from The Old Country Store for $12.95 each, plus $2.50 shipping and handling (Tennessee residents add $1.13 tax).

Fill out this order form and mail to:

The Old Country Store
56 Casey Jones Lane
Casey Jones Village
Jackson, TN 38305
(901) 668-1223
1-800-748-9588

Please send me _____ copy (copies) of **The Old Country Store Cookbook** at $12.95 each plus $2.50 postage and handling (Tennessee residents add sales tax of $1.13). Enclosed is my check or money order for $ _____ .
Make check payable to **The Old Country Store Cookbook** and mail to the above address.

Name _____
Address _____
City _____ State _____ Zip _____

MERCHANDISE ORDER FORM

Payment Method:

Personal Check _____

Money Order _____

Visa # _____
    Expires _____

Mastercard # _____
    Expires _____

American Express # _____
    Expires _____

Discover Card # _____
    Expires _____

Subtotal $ _____

TN Residents Tax $ _____
  (if applicable)

Shipping/Handling $ _____
  (per item)

TOTAL DUE $ _____

Please return page 173 **and** this form to:
  The Old Country Store
  56 Casey Jones Lane
  Jackson, TN 38305

Thanks for your order. Payable by personal check, money order, Visa, Mastercard, American Express or Discover Card.
Expect your order within 7 days of receipt. Come see us personally whenever you can.